PASSAGES
THROUGH RECOVERY

About the Author:

Terence T. Gorski, M.A., C.A.C., is a nationally recognized author, lecturer, workshop leader, and an acknowledged leader in the chemical dependency field and codependency field. His comprehensive approach to recovery, based on his nearly twenty years of clinical experience, has revolutionized the field of relapse prevention. Gorski's pioneering work in relapse prevention has helped thousands of chemically dependent people to achieve sobriety. His ability to explain complex recovery principles in an entertaining and easy-to-understand way has made him a popular public speaker. Thousands of people use his relationship-building approach in recovery. As president of The CENAPS Corporation (The Center For Applied Sciences) in Hazel Crest, Illinois, he has provided research, training, and consultation services to numerous treatment centers.

PASSAGES THROUGH RECOVERY

An Action Plan For Preventing Relapse

Terence T. Gorski

HAZELDEN®

First published June 1989.

Copyright (c) 1989, Terence T. Gorski.

ISBN: 0-89486-518-8

Library of Congress Catalog Card Number: 89-80190

Printed in the United States of America.

Editor's Note:

Hazelden Educational Materials offers a variety of information on chemical dependency and related areas. Our publica-
tions do not necessarily represent Hazelden or its programs,
nor do they officially speak for any Twelve Step organization.

The stories of recovering people presented in this book
are not based on individuals. They represent typical cases
and composite experiences. Any resemblance between any
real person and the examples used in this book is purely
coincidental.

Contents

Acknowledgments

This book is the result of nearly two decades of involvement in treating alcoholism and drug dependence. So many people have contributed to the ideas on which this book is based that I could never acknowledge them all.

The late Stan Martindale introduced me to the field of psychology and therapy. Richard Weedman, my first mentor, taught me about alcoholism and the need for long-term recovery. His encouragement and role modeling helped me through the difficult early years of my counseling career, and gave me the foundation and the courage to go on. Jim Kelleher, my first supervisor, showed me what recovery means on a personal level and encouraged me to start my own recovery.

I am grateful to Father Joseph Martin, a friend and mentor, who passed on the tradition of the Twelve Steps and helped me to develop an in-depth understanding of the wisdom that they contain.

Claudia Black helped me to a better understanding of how family of origin problems affect recovery from chemical addictions. Her insights brought greater depth and substance to the Late Recovery section of this book.

This manuscript would not have been possible without the criticism and help of my Hazelden editor, Judy Delaney. Kathy Chidichimo, Mary Johnson, and Claudia Krohn were responsible for the typing and retyping of the many drafts necessary to create the final manuscript.

Special thanks to my wife, Jan Smith, who acted as a sounding board and supported me through the writing process; to Joe Troiani, a lifelong friend who helped me keep the recovery process in perspective; and to Dr. Heidi Lord Harlow, who really didn't help with this manuscript, but I promised I would mention her so she could see her name in print.

Introduction

During the seventeen years I have been a chemical dependency counselor, I've seen the struggles of many people who were attempting to recover from this illness. Some people sought sobriety through the Twelve Step programs of Alcoholics Anonymous (A.A.) and Narcotics Anonymous (N.A.). Others turned to therapy. Many people sought the benefits of both. Still others tried to make it alone.

I saw many people succeed in finding a lasting recovery. Some had to relapse many times before they found sobriety. Others gave up in despair and eventually died from their disease.

This book is intended to show you the patterns that emerged out of the thousands of recovery stories I have seen unfold. It will also help me understand the one recovery experience I have lived, my own.

My goal is to explain my understanding of the recovery process. I want you to understand how it works, and what I think chemically dependent people need to do to move from active addiction to sobriety.

My experience as a counselor, lecturer, and workshop leader tells me that most chemically dependent people, whether they are recovering now or have relapsed over and over, will identify with a great deal of what is written here. You may relate to all or only part of it. If you do not identify with it all, simply take what fits and leave the rest.

If you or someone you know has experienced the things that I describe, it simply means you share many of the common experiences of recovery from chemical dependency.

I believe the Steps of A.A. are the single most effective tool for recovery, so I will refer to them and how I think they relate to each stage of recovery. It is my personal understanding of the Steps. I drew on wisdom shared with me by Father Joseph Martin, an internationally known lecturer and cofounder of Ashley, a large treatment center in Havre de Grace, Maryland. My association with Father Martin helped me understand the Twelve Step program better.

Now, on with the task. What is recovery?

PART I

An Overview of the Recovery Process—Learning Where We're Going

Chemical dependency is a disease that causes a person to lose control over use of alcohol or other drugs. It is an addiction. This loss of control causes physical, psychological, social, and spiritual problems. The total person is affected.

Sobriety is living a meaningful and comfortable life without the need for alcohol or other drugs. In recovery, we move from a destructive dependence on alcohol or other drugs toward full physical, psychological, social, and spiritual health. When we stop using chemicals, we begin to heal the damage to our bodies, minds, relationships, and spirit.

Sobriety is more than just healing the damage. It is living a lifestyle that promotes continued physical, psychological, social, and spiritual health.

Abstinence from mood-altering chemicals is the first requirement toward sobriety. We have to do this before we can learn what to do to get and stay healthy in all areas of our lives.

Notice that I didn't say sobriety was abstinence from alcohol and drugs. Abstinence is the beginning of sobriety. It is the ticket to get into the theater, not the movie we are going to see.

We don't recover overnight. Recovery is a *developmental* process. We go through a series of stages. The term "developmental" means to grow in stages or in steps. It is a gradual effort to learn new and progressively more complex skills. A developmental model of recovery means that we can grow from simple abstinence to a meaningful and comfortable sobriety. We confront new problems while abstinent and try to solve them. Sometimes we fail, and sometimes we succeed. Whatever the outcome, we learn from the experience and try again.

The skills necessary for long-term sobriety are all directed at finding meaning and purpose in life. Sobriety is a way of thinking, a way of acting, a way of relating to others. It is a philosophy of living. It requires the daily effort of working a recovery program.

The longer we stay sober, the more we need to know to maintain a sense of meaning, purpose, and comfort. The things we did to stay comfortable at thirty days of sobriety may no longer work for us at sixty days. It is as if the recovery process forces us to keep growing, learning, and changing.

Abstinence — a necessary first step in learning what to do to get and stay healthy in all areas of life.
Sobriety — abstinence plus a return to full physical, psychological, social, and spiritual health.

The passage toward sobriety is very clear. First, we stop using chemicals entirely. Then we begin to associate with others who want sobriety. We listen to others with more time in the Twelve Step program, and we practice what we learn in our day-to-day lives. We fail at some things and succeed at others, but we maintain a commitment to learn and grow no matter what happens. We keep what works for us and leave the rest. We talk honestly about what we tried and what happened. We learn from our experiences and share this new knowledge with others.

The Progressive Stages of Recovery

The developmental model of recovery (I will call it the DMR for short) is based upon a series of beliefs:

1. Recovery is a long-term process that is not easy.
2. Recovery requires total abstinence from alcohol and other drugs, plus active efforts toward personal growth.
3. There are underlying principles that govern the recovery process.
4. The better we understand these principles, the easier it will be for us to recover.
5. Understanding alone will not promote recovery; the new understanding must be put into action.
6. The actions that are necessary to produce full recovery can be clearly and accurately described as recovery tasks.
7. It is normal and natural to periodically get stuck on the road to recovery. *It is not whether you get stuck that determines success or failure, but it is how you cope with the stuck point that counts.*

To learn about recovery, it is helpful to divide the process into stages. We will be learning about six different stages of recovery. I will refer to these as (1) transition, (2) stabilization, (3) early recovery, (4) middle recovery, (5) late recovery, and (6) maintenance.

During the first recovery stage, *transition*, we recognize we have problems with chemicals, but we think we can solve them by learning how to control our use. This stage ends when we recognize we are not capable of control (that we are "powerless" over alcohol or other drugs), and we need to abstain to regain control of our lives. We don't yet know why we are out of control or how to stay sober; we just know we cannot continue the way we have been. In A.A. this is called "being sick and tired of being sick and tired."

During the second stage, *stabilization*, we now know we have serious problems with alcohol and drug use and that we need to stop using completely, but we are unable to do so. During this time we recuperate from acute withdrawal (the stage of shakiness and confusion that we experience as our bodies detoxify). And we recuperate from long-term or post-acute withdrawal (the period of time lasting from six to eighteen months when we feel like we are in a mental fog). During this stage we learn how to "stay away from one drink (or one dose of drugs) one day at a time."

The third stage, *early recovery*, is a time of internal change. During early recovery we learn how to become comfortably abstinent. The physical compulsion to use chemicals is relieved, and we learn more about our addiction and how it affected us. We also learn to overcome our feelings of shame, guilt, and remorse. We become capable of coping with our problems without chemical use. Early recovery ends when we are ready to begin practicing what we learned by straightening out other areas of our lives.

During *middle recovery*, the fourth stage, we learn how to repair this past damage and put balance in our lives. We learn that full recovery means "practicing these principles [the sober living skills we learned in early recovery] in all of our affairs" (in the real world of daily living). During middle recovery, we make it a priority to straighten out our relationships with people. We reevaluate our significant relationships, including our relationships with family and friends, and our careers. If we find we are unhappy in any of these areas, we admit it and make plans to do something about it. In A.A. terms, this means making amends. We acknowledge that we have done damage to other people. We become willing to take responsibility and to do whatever possible to repair it. Middle recovery ends when we have a balanced and stable life.

During the fifth stage, *late recovery*, we focus on overcoming obstacles to healthy living that we may have learned as children, before our addiction even developed. Many chemically dependent people come from dysfunctional families. Because our parents may not have done a very good job at parenting, we may never have learned the skills necessary to be happy. Late recovery ends when we have accomplished three things.

- First, we recognize the problems we have as adults that were caused by growing up in a dysfunctional family.
- Second, we learn how to recover from the unresolved pain that was caused by growing up in a dysfunctional family.
- Finally, we learn how to solve current problems in spite of the obstacles caused by how we were raised.

The sixth and final stage is *maintenance*. During maintenance, chemically dependent people learn their disease is called "alcohol-ism," not "alcohol-wasm." We recognize we have a need for continued growth and development as people. We recognize that we can never safely use alcohol and other drugs, and we must practice a daily recovery program to keep addictive thinking from returning. We live in a way that allows us to enjoy the journey of life .

Recovery Stage	Major Theme
1. Transition	Giving up the need to control alcohol and other drug use.
2. Stabilization	Recuperating from the damage caused by addictive use.
3. Early Recovery	Internal change (change of thinking, feeling, and acting related to alcohol and drug use).
4. Middle Recovery	External change (repairing the lifestyle damage caused by addictive use, and developing a balanced lifestyle).
5. Late Recovery	Growing beyond childhood limitations.
6. Maintenance	Balanced living and continued growth and development.

Many chemically dependent people ask, "What are some things I might do that would cause a relapse?" The answer is simple. You don't have to do anything. Stop using alcohol and other drugs, but continue to live your life the way you always have. Your disease will do the rest. It will trigger a series of automatic and habitual reactions to life and living that will create so much pain and discomfort that a return to chemical use will seem like a positive option.

Recovery means *change*. To change, we must have goals. To reach our goals, it helps to have an action plan or a step-by-step guide showing us what to do and how to do it. This book is designed to be such a guide.

Each of the following chapters is a detailed description of one of the recovery stages. Don't feel overwhelmed. Remember, recovery is a process of growth that takes time. To go from stabilization to maintenance may require from three to fifteen years, depending upon how sick you were when you started to recover, how hard and consistently you worked at your recovery plans, and the type of help you received from others.

This book doesn't contain a magic formula. It simply describes many things that people who have successfully recovered from chemical dependency have done. By understanding what others have done, it becomes possible to follow the advice often heard at A.A. meetings — "If you want what we got, do what we did." Please accept these descriptions in the spirit that they are offered. It is my intent to share the courage, strength, and hope of hundreds of recovering alcoholics.

Recognizing Our Teachable Moments

There was once a student who couldn't understand the solution to a complex puzzle. He went to a wise old man for instruction. After the wise old man made several attempts to explain, the student still couldn't grasp the principle. His teacher comforted him by saying: "We each have our own teachable moments. When we are ready to understand something, the understanding comes. If you cannot solve the problem now, turn your attention to a different and easier problem that will prepare you to solve the more complex problem."

I hope this book will lead you to your teachable moment. It is meant to help you determine where you are in your recovery process, and to help you set some realistic goals for further growth.

When we review each stage of the DMR, we will be looking at the Steps of A.A. that correspond to that stage. We will also be looking at a series of recovery tasks that chemical dependency counselors developed to support our A.A. program. It's important to remember that each task is completed on two levels. The first is on *the level of experience:*

- "I have experienced and felt the real need for this."

The second is on *the level of conscious understanding:*

- "I am able to describe and explain to others what these Steps or tasks are all about."

At first we are unable to explain what we are experiencing. We lack the words or the language of sobriety to fully understand what has happened. But because people who are more knowledgeable in recovery than we are can guide us, we follow directions and things begin to make sense.

PART II

Transition — Giving Up the Need to Control Use

We need to accomplish three major things during Transition:

- We recognize that we have lost control over our alcohol and other drug use.
- We recognize that we can't control our use because we are addicted.
- We make a commitment to a program of recovery that includes the help of others.

Let's look at these three goals in more detail.

Recognizing Loss of Control

Transition begins when progressive life problems caused by the addiction force us to recognize that we are in trouble, but we are not yet convinced that the problems are related to alcohol and drug use. As a result, we try to solve these problems without doing anything about our use of alcohol and drugs. Although we may make temporary progress, in the long run these efforts fail. Why? Because the life problems are really being caused by our alcohol and other drug use. Until we understand this vital fact, we can't make any real progress. Our failure, however, serves a purpose. It forces us to look at the relationship between our problems and our alcohol and other drug use.

- First, we might attempt to solve our problems without taking our chemical use into consideration.
- We fail over and over to solve our problems this way.
- Finally, we are forced to recognize that our alcohol and other drug use is causing the problems. We gradually learn that our ordinary skills in problem solving will not work in trying to solve problems caused by our use of chemicals.

When we finally see a relationship between our chemical use and our life problems, we don't say, "I am chemically dependent." This generally doesn't happen until later. What we do say is, "I am a social drinker with problems," or "I am a recreational drug user with problems." We still believe that we are "responsible users" who have life problems. We say to ourselves: *I use alcohol and other drugs because I have life problems. If the problems would go away, I would be able to stop using.*

If we find help in sorting out what is really going on, most of us recognize that our chemical use is causing the problems. Many of us stubbornly hold on to the belief that when we straighten out our lives, we will be able to drink and use again. This secret belief often leads us to relapse later in recovery.

Attempts to Control Use

When we realize that we are having problems caused by our chemical use, most of us ask ourselves: *How can I continue to use alcohol and other drugs but avoid the problems?* The solution seems easy. We simply try to control our drinking and using. During this stage, our purpose is to try to prove we are recreational or social users by struggling to control our use.

At this point, most of us are not yet willing to give up our substance. We really see no reason to do so. Why should we? We believe we are social users who can control our use. We believe we can handle it. Besides, we don't really know what we would do without it. We often say things like, "I don't *need* it, you understand; I just happen to really like alcohol and drugs."

Even though we don't believe we are addicted, we are smart enough at this point to recognize that our use of alcohol and other drugs is hurting us, and that we need to do something about it.

The plan to handle these problems seems remarkably simple. "I simply won't use as much alcohol or drugs as I used to," or "I won't use as often as I used to," or "I won't get as drunk or stoned as I used to." The problem is we don't define how much is "too much" or how often is "too often" or how drunk is "too drunk."

Our efforts fail again and again. Eventually, we came to believe that we couldn't control our alcohol and other drug use and there was a bigger problem. We were out of control. If we knew that chemical dependency or addiction was a disease, we would begin to understand that our illness makes it impossible for us to control our use. But most of us were not open to new learning at that time. Even if we were forced into treatment or to attend a DUI school, we were experts at kidding ourselves. We had a million ways to convince ourselves that this information about addiction didn't apply to us. We said: "This addiction is a terrible thing. If I ever got addicted, I would get help. Thank God that I am not that bad and can still handle my problems by myself."

Most chemically dependent people attempt a series of predictable strategies in order to regain control. The most common are:

1. *Changing the pace.* The first attempt is simply to slow down. We still drink or use as much, but we attempt to pace ourselves. We attempt to go easy.

2. *Cutting the quantity.* We try to restrict or cut down on how much we use. We still use with the same frequency. We just try to use less.

3. *Restricting the time of day.* We try to restrict the times we use. For example, we don't start until after 6:00 P.M. or after 10:00 P.M. We stop using in the morning, or at lunch, or in the afternoon.

4. *Changing the frequency.* We try to change how often we drink or use. For example, we refuse to drink Monday through Thursday. We only use marijuana on Saturday night. We don't use alcohol and drugs after 5:00 P.M. on Sunday so we can "get it together" to go to work on Monday.

5. *Changing the kind of drugs we use.* We change the kind of alcohol or other drugs we use. We believe it isn't the *use* that is causing problems, it is the kind of drug we're using. For example, we switch from bourbon to wine, then wine to beer. We swear off cocaine and only use marijuana. Maybe we stop drinking and get a prescription for Librium or Valium.

6. *Using other drugs to help control.* We often begin to use one drug to attempt to control the effects of another. We may take diet pills or amphetamines before using alcohol in order to keep from getting drunk. We may take Librium the morning after to eliminate the shakes so we can go to work. We may smoke marijuana for the first three hours of a party so we won't drink as much. This pattern of use is often called "mixing and matching."

7. *Becoming temporarily abstinent.* When all else fails we try temporary periods of abstinence. The goal isn't to learn how to live a sober life; the goal is to get strong enough to be able to successfully control our use later. We recognize our drug use is making us sick or wearing us down, so we take a rest from it. We temporarily go on the wagon. We can often convince ourselves that we didn't have a problem in the first place.

In order to recover, we need to shift our belief system from "I am a social drinker (recreational drug user) who is capable of control" to "I am an addicted user who cannot control." Once this recognition occurs, treatment can be effective.

Recognition of Our Illness

It is not enough to know that we have lost control; we must also know about the disease of addiction that has caused us to lose control. Furthermore, we must know about the steps necessary for recovery.

First, we must learn the basics about addiction. Second, we must analyze our presenting problems and their relationship to alcohol and drug use. Third, we must decide if we are addicted. Fourth, we need to examine our ways of denying our addiction to be sure that we are being honest with ourselves. Finally, we need to take the first three Steps of the Twelve Step program. Let's look at each of these in more detail.

Learning the Basics about Addiction

Addiction is a physical disease similar to cancer and heart disease, in that it is chronic and must be managed. It is highly possible that some people are genetically predisposed to becoming addicted and respond differently to alcohol and drug use than people who aren't. All that is necessary for those people to become addicted is to begin using alcohol and other drugs, even if moderately at first. The biochemistry of addiction will do the rest!

People do not become chemically dependent simply because they have psychological or emotional problems or because they come from dysfunctional families. But some people who have psychological and emotional problems are more reluctant to seek help and require more intensive treatment in order to recover.

To be addicted is neither right nor wrong, it simply is. People who suffer from addiction are not at fault any more than someone who has heart disease, cancer, or diabetes. Addiction is a no-fault illness. To believe that we developed it because there is something wrong or defective about ourselves will simply create the shame and the guilt that may drive us back to drinking. (But we *are* responsible for what we do about it once we've admitted we're sick and know that help is available.)

Chemical dependency is a disease. It slowly and predictably develops and progresses over time. It is a chronic, lifelong illness. It does not go away. No matter how long the chemically dependent person is abstinent, the changes in the brain and nervous system that act as the foundation of the disease do not go away. Many scientists believe the disease progresses even when people are abstinent. People who have been abstinent for periods of ten years or longer often find that if they drink again, they don't start up where they left off; they are much worse.

Chemical dependency is eventually fatal. If we continue to put alcohol or other drugs into our bodies, we will die. It's just that simple. If we want to live, we must stop using alcohol and other drugs. If we want to die, all we have to do is start using again.

Chemical dependency produces self-defeating habits of thinking, managing feelings, emotions, and behavior. Even though we are abstinent, these self-defeating habits will stay with us unless we change them by working the Twelve Steps, going into counseling, or both.

Chemical dependency damages our social life. People who are involved in committed relationships with us are changed because of our chemical dependency. The stress which they experience while living in a relationship with us while we are actively using creates serious problems for them. Their response to these problems in a specific, predictable pattern of

16

behavior is called *codependency*. Recovery, therefore, will require the involvement of the entire family to be most effective.

Chemical dependency is progressive. The early stages of chemical dependency are marked by our growing dependency on alcohol and other drugs. We need these drugs to feel good about ourselves and other people. The middle stage is marked by a progressive loss of control. We begin drinking (or using other drugs) more than we want to, getting intoxicated when we choose not to, and drinking more frequently than we desire. The final stage is marked by degeneration. We become physically, psychologically, socially, and spiritually sick.

If you have been in a chemical dependency treatment facility, you have probably attended sessions where you learned these things. If you haven't or have questions about this information, the book that I wrote with Merlene Miller, *Learning to Live Again — A Guide to Recovery from Alcoholism,* and the book, *Under the Influence,* by James Milam and Katherine Ketcham, may be helpful.

Analyzing Your Presenting Problems

Presenting problems are the things that are going wrong in our lives that motivated us to seek treatment for alcoholism. Our drinking has probably caused problems with family, friends, work, finances, or perhaps even the law. These problems are so severe that we know we have to do something, but nothing we do seems to work.

To explore these problems, take a sheet of paper. Draw a line down the middle of the page, dividing it into two columns. On the top of the first column, write the word *Problem.* At the top of the second column, write the words *Relationship to Alcohol and Other Drug Use.*

In the first column, write a list of all of the major problems you now have or did have in your life. Make sure each one is written in a complete sentence.

In the second column, directly across from each problem, write how the problem relates to alcohol and drug use. There are three possible relationships:

1. The alcohol and drugs could directly cause your problem. (I drink or use drugs, and that causes problems.)
2. You drink or use to escape your problems. (My problems are so stressful that I use alcohol and drugs to cope.)
3. Alcohol and drugs could make already existing problems worse. (I have a problem: I drink in an effort to cope with it. The drinking makes the problem worse.)

Here's an example of what you might write:

Problem:	*Relationship to Alcohol and Other Drug Use:*
1. I have job problems because I am often late, and I am making a lot of mistakes.	1 - a. I am late for work because I have a hangover from drinking. 1 - b. I make mistakes because I am hung over, or I'm eager to leave so I can get a drink.
2. My wife wants a divorce because I get angry, hit her and the kids, and I am seldom home.	2 - a. I get angry because she complains about my drinking. 2 - b. I only hit her when I am drunk or really hung over. 2 - c. I leave her at home because she won't go with me to bars and she doesn't like my drinking friends.
3. My brother won't talk to me, and he doesn't invite us over anymore.	3. He is still angry because I got drunk at his daughter's graduation party. I made a fool of myself and embarrassed him and his daughter.
4. I am broke. I just can't keep money in my pocket.	4 - a. I spend more money on drinking than I should. 4 - b. I spend too much on luxury items to try and make up for not being home.

Deciding If You Are Addicted

If you are exploring your chemical use for the first time, now you must decide how much of the information about addiction applies to you. This is an important decision you shouldn't have to make alone. You would probably want to find a certified alcohol and drug abuse counselor or an A.A. sponsor to help you. What follows are twelve questions (developed from the *DSM-III-R** criteria for substance dependence) many counselors use in order to evaluate if a person is chemically dependent. Take a pen or pencil and see how you fare.

YES NO Do you ever use alcohol or drugs in larger quantities than you intended?

YES NO Do you ever use alcohol or drugs for longer periods of time than you intended?

YES NO Do you now or have you had in the past a persistent desire to cut down or control your alcohol and drug use?

YES NO Have you ever tried to cut down or control your use?

YES NO Do you spend more time than you should in getting ready to use, using, or recovering from using?

YES NO Have you ever failed to meet a major life responsibility because you were intoxicated, hung over, or in withdrawal?

YES NO Have you given up any work, social, or recreational activities because of alcohol or drug use?

YES NO Have you had any physical, psychological, or social problems that were caused by or made worse by your alcohol or drug use?

---

* The questions are based on information in the *Diagnostic and Statistical Manual for Mental Disorders, Third Edition, Revised,* Copyright 1987, American Psychiatric Association.

YES NO   Have you continued to use alcohol or drugs in spite of knowing that they were causing or making physical, psychological, or social problems worse?

YES NO   Did your tolerance (your ability to use a lot of alcohol or drugs without feeling intoxicated) increase radically after you started to use?

YES NO   Did you ever get physically uncomfortable or sick on the day after using alcohol or other drugs?

YES NO   Have you ever used alcohol or other drugs to keep you from getting sick or to make a hangover go away?

If you answered yes to three or more of these questions, you are probably chemically dependent. If you answered yes to six or more, you are definitely chemically dependent. If you answered yes to nine or more, you are in an advanced stage of your chemical dependency.

Identifying Your Denial Patterns

The first time most people answer a questionnaire like the one you just completed, they try to talk themselves out of answering the questions honestly. This is normal. It's called denial.

Most of us use denial to protect ourselves from the awareness that we are addicted. In its simplest form, denial is a lack of information. We experience symptoms we don't understand, so we push them out of our thoughts. Denial can become conscious suppression. We know we are experiencing something painful, but we consciously push it from our mind because of shame, guilt, or unwillingness to look at what's causing the pain. In its most severe form, denial becomes unconscious repression — chronically being unaware of the pain. We simply refuse to acknowledge the pain. As a result, we experience painful and unwanted symptoms with no idea where they came from.

There are three levels of denial.

- Mild denial — lack of information needed to understand what is happening.
- Moderate denial — consciously pushing unwanted memories from the mind.
- Severe denial — unconsciously repressing the memory. Adverse symptoms are present when a person has no idea of what is causing the symptoms.

It's important to identify how you deny or used to deny the reality of your addiction. The following questionnaire can help you identify the common denial patterns that most alcoholics use. Key phrases can help you to recognize your own denial patterns. Answer both questions that follow, using these definitions to guide you.

In answering the question — *How often do you use this form of denial?* — use the following definitions:

Never	= I don't use it at all.
Sometimes	= I use it once a week or less.
Often	= I use it about once a day.
Very Often	= I use it many times during the day.

In answering the question — *How strong is it (my denial pattern)?* — use these definitions:

Very Strong	= It's difficult to talk me out of my denial even with a lot of effort.
Strong	= I'm committed to my denial pattern, but I can be talked out of it with a reasonable effort.
Weak	= It's somewhat easy to talk me out of denial.
Very Weak	= It's very easy to talk me out of my denial.

1. *Absolute denial.* "No, not me. I don't have a problem."

   A. How often do you use it?
   ☐ Never ☐ Sometimes ☐ Often ☐ Very Often
   B. How strong is it?
   ☐ Very Strong ☐ Strong ☐ Weak ☐ Very Weak

2. *Minimizing.* "My drinking isn't that bad. I know it is a problem, but it just isn't as serious as people think."

   A. How often do you use it?
   ☐ Never ☐ Sometimes ☐ Often ☐ Very Often
   B. How strong is it?
   ☐ Very Strong ☐ Strong ☐ Weak ☐ Very Weak

3. *Avoidance by omission.* "I won't talk about it. I will talk about everything else, but I will not talk about my drinking."

   A. How often do you use it?
   ☐ Never ☐ Sometimes ☐ Often ☐ Very Often
   B. How strong is it?
   ☐ Very Strong ☐ Strong ☐ Weak ☐ Very Weak

4. *Avoidance deluge.* "I'll talk about everything else except my alcoholism, and I will immobilize you with tons of garbage."

   A. How often do you use it?
   ☐ Never ☐ Sometimes ☐ Often ☐ Very Often
   B. How strong is it?
   ☐ Very Strong ☐ Strong ☐ Weak ☐ Very Weak

5. *Avoidance uproar.* "I'll create a crisis situation for you if you push me into talking about my drinking."

   A. How often do you use it?

   ☐ Never ☐ Sometimes ☐ Often ☐ Very Often

   B. How strong is it?

   ☐ Very Strong ☐ Strong ☐ Weak ☐ Very Weak

6. *Scapegoating.* "I only use alcohol and drugs because of my wife. If you were married to a woman like her, or if you had a job like I have, you would drink as much as I do." "If it were not for my boss, I wouldn't be drinking that much." "If you were a good therapist, I'd be able to stop."

   A. How often do you use it?

   ☐ Never ☐ Sometimes ☐ Often ☐ Very Often

   B. How strong is it?

   ☐ Very Strong ☐ Strong ☐ Weak ☐ Very Weak

7. *Rationalizing.* "When confronted about my alcohol and drug use problems, I can talk myself and other people around in circles with my reasons for it."

   A. How often do you use it?

   ☐ Never ☐ Sometimes ☐ Often ☐ Very Often

   B. How strong is it?

   ☐ Very Strong ☐ Strong ☐ Weak ☐Very Weak

8. *Intellectualizing.* "The problem of abusive drinking and alcoholism goes back to our sociocultural, blah, blah, blah."

   A. How often do you use it?

   ☐ Never ☐ Sometimes ☐ Often ☐ Very Often

   B. How strong is it?

   ☐ Very Strong ☐ Strong ☐ Weak ☐ Very Weak

9. *Comparison.* "I don't drink as much as my boss does and he's not in trouble. I know Uncle Charlie, who used to drink two fifths a day, and he died of old age."

   A. How often do you use it?
   ☐ Never ☐ Sometimes ☐ Often ☐ Very Often
   B. How strong is it?
   ☐ Very Strong ☐ Strong ☐ Weak ☐ Very Weak

10. *Diagnosis of yourself as beyond help.* "I've gone too far to get any help. How can you expect a dilapidated old drunk like me to change his habits?"

    A. How often do you use it?
    ☐ Never ☐ Sometimes ☐ Often ☐ Very Often
    B. How strong is it?
    ☐ Very Strong ☐ Strong ☐ Weak ☐ Very Weak

11. *Flight into health.* "I've been sober for twenty-five minutes now, and I understand what my problem is and it is solved. I know too much to ever drink again."

    A. How often do you use it?
    ☐ Never ☐ Sometimes ☐ Often ☐ Very Often
    B. How strong is it?
    ☐ Very Strong ☐ Strong ☐ Weak ☐ Very Weak

12. *Consequential sobriety.* "I can't drink ever again, because I'll get sick and die. These consequences will scare me into permanent sobriety. Since I know how awful my life will be if I continue to drink, I won't drink anymore, and since I know I won't drink anymore, I don't need treatment."

    A. How often do you use it?
    ☐ Never ☐ Sometimes ☐ Often ☐ Very Often
    B. How strong is it?
    ☐ Very Strong ☐ Strong ☐ Weak ☐ Very Weak

13. *Compliance.* "I'll do whatever you say if you get off my back. I'll get well by doing what you say, ha, ha, ha."

   A. How often do you use it?

   ☐ Never ☐ Sometimes ☐ Often ☐ Very Often

   B. How strong is it?

   ☐ Very Strong ☐ Strong ☐ Weak ☐ Very Weak

14. *Manipulation.* "I'll let you help me if you do it for me. If you make me do things I don't want to do, I'll end up getting drunk."

   A. How often do you use it?

   ☐ Never ☐ Sometimes ☐ Often ☐ Very Often

   B. How strong is it?

   ☐ Very Strong ☐ Strong ☐ Weak ☐ Very Weak

15. *The democratic disease state.* "I have a right to continue to drink myself to death, even if I am an alcoholic and even if I die."

   A. How often do you use it?

   ☐ Never ☐ Sometimes ☐ Often ☐ Very Often

   B. How strong is it?

   ☐ Very Strong ☐ Strong ☐ Weak ☐ Very Weak

Taking the Steps of A.A.

During transition, most chemically dependent people experientially but unconsciously work the first three Steps of A.A. In transition, we experience that we are powerless over alcohol and drugs. As a result, we experience unmanageable lives. We need to find help from a Power greater than ourselves and actively seek to find someone or something that can help us. We also need to become willing to receive help.

The First Step

After analyzing our alcohol and drug use history, we become ready to consciously take the First Step of Alcoholics Anonymous.

Step 1: We admitted we were powerless over alcohol — that our lives had become unmanageable.[1]

There are instructions of how to take a formal First Step in the Big Book of Alcoholics Anonymous. Or you may want to read the pamphlet, *Step One: The Foundation of Recovery*,[2] which explains how to take the First Step.

A simple way to take a First Step is to write a list of all the reasons why you believe you are powerless over alcohol and drugs, and to write a list of all of the problems that alcohol and other drug use have caused you.

When these are written out, reviewed with a counselor, and discussed in support groups or at Twelve Step meetings, they are effective at helping people recognize their addiction to chemicals. In my experience, about 80 percent of chemically dependent people who have examined their use of alcohol or other drugs this way (while they were not using) clearly recognized their addiction. It's not an easy process, but it does help people become consciously aware that they are addicted.

When we make a decision to stop using alcohol and other drugs, we have begun to take the First Step of Alcoholics Anonymous.

Recognizing the Need for Help

The transition stage of recovery ends when we recognize on some level that we need help and ask for it from someone who

---

1. Reprinted with permission of A.A. World Services, Inc., New York, N.Y. The Twelve Steps of A.A. appear in Appendix One.

2. William Springborn, *Step One: The Foundation of Recovery* (Center City, Minn: Hazelden Educational Materials, 1985).

knows about chemical dependency and recovery.

At some point during the transition stage, we have accepted our need for abstinence, but we have not accepted that we need the help of others. The reasoning goes something like this: "I know I can't handle the alcohol and the drugs so I need to stop. Therefore, I'll stop. I have willpower, and I'll be able to stay off of this with my own resources." But this approach usually fails.

We can't do it alone. The simple truth is we need help to recover. After a series of attempts and failures, most of us get the point. We recognize that we need help and are willing to seek it out and accept it when it is offered. This acceptance of the need for help is critical.

It is the repeated failure to stay sober on our own that forces us to look at the Second Step.

Step 2: Came to believe that a Power greater than ourselves could restore us to sanity.

In other words, we recognize that there is something seriously wrong with us, and that we cannot understand or correct the problem by ourselves. We need the help of someone or something that is stronger, smarter, and bigger than we are.

The type of help we seek at this point is critical. It is important for people who are concerned about their alcohol and other drug use to seek help from someone who is knowledgeable in chemical dependency. Not all psychiatrists, physicians, psychologists, social workers, and clergypeople understand what chemical addiction is. Many still believe that controlled drinking is possible once the underlying problems that caused the addiction are identified and corrected. Nothing could be further from the truth. We must seek the help of knowledgeable professionals and other recovering people. Here is the process we go through in learning to accept the help of others.

- Recognition of the problems caused by alcohol and other drug use.
- Recognition of the need for abstinence.
- Recognition of the need for help.

Our primary job during this stage is to become willing to give up alcohol and drug use and to seek the help of others in staying sober. At this point, most of us don't fully understand why we need to do this. We only know that we have tried everything in our power to control our chemical use and have failed miserably. Alcoholics Anonymous calls it "hitting bottom." We now need to find a way to live a meaningful and comfortable life without alcohol or drugs.

The Steps and recovery tasks must be completed both experientially and consciously. We can *experience* something many times without ever becoming consciously aware of what is happening or why. Many of us try to control our alcohol and drug use and fail because we never come up with the obvious solution — I am powerless over alcohol and drugs. I cannot control my use no matter how hard I try. With *conscious awareness* we know what is happening. We are able to describe in words what is wrong. We can say, "I am alcoholic and my life has become unmanageable because I cannot control my alcohol and drug use." We can then figure out what to do to get sober.

How the First Three Steps Work

At the end of transition, most of us begin sorting through Steps One, Two, and Three. These Steps can be described in a shorthand form:

Step One: I can't.
Step Two: Somebody else can.
Step Three: I'll let them do it.

Step One: I Can't

There are two parts to Step One. The first part acknowledges powerlessness over alcohol and other drugs. The second part acknowledges that because of alcohol and other drug use we have become unable to manage many areas of our own life.

In Narcotics Anonymous, the First Step was modified slightly to read, "We admitted that we were powerless over our addiction, that our lives had become unmanageable."[3] I like the way this is expressed. We are not just powerless over alcohol and the drugs we consume, we are powerless over all aspects of our addiction. We need to recover physically, psychologically, socially, and spiritually.

In discussing the First Step with recovering people, I often paraphrase it this way: "I can't recover from my addiction alone; I need the help of others. I cannot reconstruct my life all by myself."

Step Two: Somebody Else Can

Step Two uses the word "sanity." If we need to be restored to "sanity," it must mean that our addiction has made us insane. What does *insanity* mean? To me, insanity means that we are not capable of using our mind in normal ways. Healthy people use their minds to think clearly and rationally, to become aware of and appropriately manage their feelings and emotions, and to behave in positive ways. They refrain from acting out in self-defeating ways. The Second Step tells us that something has damaged our ability to think rationally, manage our feelings and emotions, and responsibly regulate our behavior. That something is our addiction.

Father Martin describes sane persons as people who prepare before they act and evaluate when they're done. In other

---

3. Adapted from the Twelve Steps of Alcoholics Anonymous and reprinted with permission of A.A. World Services, Inc., New York, N.Y.

words, they get ready, they act, and then they evaluate how well it went. Target shooters state it very simply: "Ready, aim, fire."

People suffering from addictive insanity conduct life a little differently. The procedure seems to be: act impulsively, regret what they have done, and blame someone else for it. In marksmen terms, it might be stated "ready, fire, blow off your foot, aim, and blame somebody else."

The Second Step tells us that help is available from a Higher Power and from other people. It can lead us to believe, *people with more experience in sobriety in a Twelve Step program can think more clearly and rationally about addiction than I can. They can give me lifesaving information. These people understand the feelings and emotions I am experiencing as a result of my addiction. They can help me learn emotional maturity. But there is one thing other people cannot give me, and that is the courage, strength, and hope to recover. To find this, I must turn to a Higher Power, the God of my understanding.*

Step Three: I'll Let Them Do It

Step Three tells us that we must become willing. We must be willing not only to ask for help but also to follow directions. When we turn our will over to someone else, it means that we follow directions whether we feel like it or not. We find an expert, the expert tells us to do something, and we do it. Learning how to follow instructions from experts is an important part of recovery. It means we must be willing to reorganize our lives around different principles, the principles of recovery.

Step 3: Made a decision to turn our will and our lives over to the care of God *as we understood Him*.

For the active addict, the addiction is their "god." We turn something into a god when we make it the central focus of our lives and invest large amounts of time, energy, and resources into maintaining that thing, person, or object as most important in our lives. For the alcoholic or other drug addict, alcohol and drugs fit this description. We centered our lives around getting ready to use alcohol or drugs, using, and recovering from the damage done by the use so we could get ready to use again. We valued what drinking and drugging did for us. We believed that alcohol and other drug use could be our salvation. We invested large amounts of time, energy, money, and personal resources into our drinking and drugging. Very often, we were willing to give up other important areas of our lives in order to keep our addiction alive.

I often paraphrase Step Three by saying, "I'll ask for help and be willing to follow directions."

PART III

Stabilization — Recuperating from the Damage of Addiction

Four important things happen during the Stabilization stage of recovery.

- We physically recover from our withdrawal from chemical use.
- We stop being preoccupied with chemicals.
- We learn to solve problems without using alcohol or other drugs.
- We develop hope and motivation.

Let's look at each of these in more detail.

Recovery from Physical Withdrawal

At the beginning of the stabilization period, we are still using alcohol or other drugs. We want to stop, but when we try we may become physically sick. That sickness is called *withdrawal*.

There are two types of physical withdrawal — *acute (short-term) and post-acute (long-term)*. When we attempt to stop drinking and using, we may experience the severe symptoms caused by acute withdrawal. These symptoms last for one to ten days. Post-acute withdrawal symptoms, by contrast, will plague us for another six to eighteen months.

Some people in acute withdrawal seek treatment; others tough it out. Acute withdrawal usually requires medical supervision found in treatment programs. People recover from acute withdrawal in three to ten days. When acute withdrawal is over, we may think we have it made. *The worst is over. The rest of recovery will be easy.* This is true for some, but more than half of us are in for a surprise. The surprise is called post-acute withdrawal.

Post-acute withdrawal symptoms include difficulty in

- thinking clearly,
- managing feelings and emotions,
- avoiding accidents,
- managing stress,
- remembering things, or
- sleeping restfully.

At times of low stress, the symptoms are much less pronounced. During periods of high stress, the symptoms come back with a vengeance. If we don't know about post-acute withdrawal, it is easy to believe we are crazy. We feel fine one minute, but then a stressful situation comes up, and our brains check out to lunch. Many recovering people describe themselves as being in "a toxic fog." If we are under stress for long periods of time, we can become accident prone, suffer from insomnia, and eventually collapse physically or emotionally.

Most recovering people are not prepared for these symptoms. No one has ever told them about post-acute withdrawal. They think that after a couple of weeks their brains have returned to normal. They think these other symptoms must mean they are crazy or not working their programs properly.

These symptoms have been called by many names. In A.A., they are sometimes called "a dry drunk" or "white knuckle sobriety." Many doctors call it being "toxic" or "having a toxic brain" or "reversible brain dysfunction." When the symptoms get out of control, they are often called "relapse warning signs" or "building up to drink."

Whatever you call the symptoms, it's important to recognize that most, if not all, people recovering from chemical dependency experience these symptoms. It seems a rule of thirds applies. Approximately one-third of all chemically dependent people have *very mild* post-acute withdrawal. The symptoms are present, but they are minor. They are experienced as a nuisance that can be easily overcome with a little extra effort. The symptoms are easily managed with no threat to sobriety.

Another one-third of recovering people have *moderate* post-acute withdrawal. These people feel fine during periods of low stress. As stress increases, however, the symptoms begin to emerge. If the stress gets bad enough, they can lose their ability to be honest. During these periods of high stress, there is an increased risk of relapse.

The final one-third of recovering people have *severe* post-acute withdrawal. Their brains are so toxic from the aftereffects of chronic alcohol and drug poisoning that they can't think clearly, manage their emotions, or remember things, even under low stress. Their ability to be honest is minimal. Even during times of low stress, they find they can't organize their thinking, and their emotions are either overreactive or numb. These people are the most relapse prone.

Treating Post-Acute Withdrawal

The Twelve Step program of A.A. uses three primary tools to help the alcoholic through this period of recovery:

- meeting attendance,
- sponsorship, and
- slogans.

It is suggested that the new member of A.A. or N.A. attend ninety meetings in ninety days. This recommendation is designed to put us in daily contact with other sober people. We are also instructed to get a sponsor. A sponsor is someone who is more knowledgeable in the program and has a longer period of sobriety than we do. The sponsor assures us one-to-one contact with someone who can provide help during the rough times.

The new member is also taught a number of slogans such as Easy Does It, One Day at a Time, Live and Let Live, There Is No Problem So Bad that a Drink Won't Make It Worse, and Turn It Over and Leave It There. These slogans are designed to interrupt addictive thinking. In A.A., stress management is described by the acronym "HALT." Recovering people are told not to get too hungry, angry, lonely, or tired. Poor nutrition, emotionally intense situations, social isolation, and fatigue all create stress. And stress aggravates post-acute withdrawal. The lower the stress, the less severe the symptoms.

A.A. helps people stabilize with three primary tools: meeting attendance, sponsorship, and slogans.

People who stay sober long enough to stabilize seem to use a set of principles to help them manage post-acute withdrawal. The most common are:

1. Recognize that post-acute withdrawal results from the long-term effects of chronic alcohol and drug poisoning to the brain. These are physical symptoms that can be treated. Don't feel ashamed or guilty about the symptoms or be afraid to seek help.
2. Pay attention to the symptoms. Learn how to recognize when you are confused or mismanaging feelings and emotions or overreacting to stress.
3. Come to understand that these symptoms are part of the disease of addiction. They are signs that your brain is not functioning normally because it was poisoned by alcohol and drugs, possibly for many years.

4. Talk openly about these symptoms with others and receive feedback. It's very comforting to talk with people who have experienced these symptoms and learned how to successfully manage them.

5. Keep your time filled with recovery activities so that you are never too far away from a meeting or someone you can talk to. In that way, if the symptoms begin to get worse, you are close to a source of help.

6. Recognize the importance of diet. Most recovering people are malnourished when they stop using chemicals, and continue to be malnourished because they have poor diets in recovery. Eating three well-balanced meals a day can minimize post-acute withdrawal symptoms. Don't get hooked into fad diets or megavitamin therapy. Ask your doctor or a trained dietician to recommend a proper diet and vitamin supplements that will provide sufficient nutrition to allow your brain and nervous system to heal.

7. Avoid excessive use of caffeine or any use of nicotine if possible. Heavy caffeine (more than five cups per day) or any regular nicotine use can aggravate the symptoms. Since both nicotine and caffeine are mood-altering drugs, it is possible to become addicted to them, not to mention the health hazards of smoking. If you believe you are drinking too much coffee and can't cut back or stop tobacco use, talk to a counselor to get some help.

8. Get plenty of sleep each night and engage in regular periods of relaxation and meditation. If you can't relax or sleep well, check out your use of caffeine and nicotine. Smoking and drinking a lot of coffee or colas can interfere with sleep and rest.

9. Engage in regular aerobic exercise for a period of thirty minutes at least three to four times a week. Get your doctor to prescribe an exercise program that is safe and takes your current physical condition into account.

10. Talk on a regular, if not daily, basis with your sponsor or a counselor about the symptoms you are experiencing, and how you are managing them. This allows you to keep your perspective as you monitor progress and problems. If you don't have a sponsor, make it a priority to get one, in addition to professional counseling if needed.
11. Learn stress management techniques. Under high stress, the symptoms of post-acute withdrawal get worse. At times of low stress, they get better. Therefore, stress management is important. Most certified alcohol and drug abuse counselors can suggest stress management techniques that work.

Stopping Our Preoccupation with Chemicals

Craving is a serious problem for most of us during the stabilization period. It's a problem for people addicted to all mood-altering chemicals, but it is especially severe among those of us who were addicted to cocaine. Craving is a result of our continuing preoccupation with our addiction.

We think about alcohol and drug use when it would be better to think about other things. This preoccupation must be broken before we can make progress in recovery. Many of us find we have gotten into the habit of "addictive thinking." Addictive thinking causes us to think self-destructive thoughts, experience painful and unmanageable feelings, and distort our memories even though we are not using. Addictive thinking also causes us to put ourselves into high-risk situations, such as visiting bars or missing meetings.

Members of A.A. often say that there are two problems — the drinking problem and the thinking problem. The drinking (or other drug use) has damaged the brain to the point where it is difficult for us to think normally. We have become preoccupied with self-defeating thoughts that will get us drunk unless we do something about them.

This preoccupation can make us incapable of being honest. To understand why, we have to become aware of our addictive preoccupation. Addictive preoccupation can be a combination of six things:

- euphoric recall,
- positive expectancy,
- a trigger event,
- obsession,
- compulsion, and
- craving.

Euphoric recall is the process of consciously focusing on and exaggerating the good memories of alcohol and other drug use while blocking out the bad memories. Euphoric recall allows us to believe we mostly had good experiences when we were using chemicals, when in reality we didn't. I often call it the "Good Old Days Syndrome."

One recovering person named Joe put it this way:

> In early recovery I would constantly think about the good old days. I'd constantly talk about how good drinking and drugging used to be. I'd focus on the good times. I knew I couldn't safely drink, and I felt that was a bad thing. How can life possibly have any meaning if I can't have all the good things that go along with drinking?

But most of Joe's good memories pertaining to drinking experiences were exaggerated. He blocked out the pain that accompanies those memories.

We can end this euphoric recall by becoming rigorously honest about our past experiences. It means being willing to reconstruct our chemical use history in detail, and telling our story to other people. It also means being willing to challenge the accuracy of our memories. In counseling, Joe initially described the following experience with alcohol as being positive.

Joe remembered an evening when he came home from work and was very tired. His wife wanted him to attend a party, and he really didn't want to go. They had an argument, and he decided to go simply to end the conflict. He felt tired and depressed. He got to the party and began to drink. Within a few minutes, his depression lifted and he became the life of the party. He flirted with other women and started having fun. When his wife became embarrassed and wanted to leave, he told her to go home by herself. The next thing he remembered was waking up the next morning at home in his own bed alone. It was 11:00 A.M. and his wife was downstairs going about her daily routine.

The first time Joe told me this story he laughed about it and said what a good time he had. "If it weren't for the drinking, I never would have enjoyed myself."

We then looked back and discussed this incident in detail. The evening started with Joe arguing with his wife. He viewed that as negative. He then backed down from the argument because he felt guilty about his past alcohol and drug use behaviors. That was a negative. He then went to a party that he didn't want to attend. That, too, was a negative. He then began to drink, and he experienced the euphoric effect of the alcohol. That was the only positive in the evening. He then began engaging in inappropriate behavior that embarrassed his wife to the point where she left the party without him. That's a negative. He then went into a blackout and doesn't remember what he did. He was flirting with a woman and may have had an affair with her, but he doesn't remember. His car was at home and he thinks he drove it, but he's not sure. He probably drove drunk and doesn't even remember. Those, too, are negatives.

When we consciously explored each event of the evening, 90 percent of them were negative. Upon consciously reexperiencing what happened and putting it into perspective, Joe realized it really wasn't a good time after all. His perception of "the good old days" changed radically.

40

When we are using euphoric recall, we truly believe that the majority of time we spent drinking and using was positive. We truly believe there were benefits. Since we have deluded ourselves that alcohol and drug use brought us pain-free pleasure in the past, it's only "reasonable" to believe that it will again bring us pain-free pleasure in the future. This belief is called *positive expectancy*. Positive expectancy sets the stage for obsession.

High risk factors—such as being around people who are using alcohol or other drugs, having an unexpected argument with our boss, or having an especially stressful day at work—make people vulnerable to *trigger events*. A trigger event is anything that causes sudden stress, pain, or discomfort. The less high risk factors in people's lives, the greater the stressor required to trigger internal dysfunction. The more high risk factors, the smaller the trigger event required.

Once a trigger event occurs, a person develops symptoms of internal dysfunction. These symptoms include difficulty in thinking clearly, managing feelings and emotions, and remembering things. There is a tendency to overreact to stress, have difficulty sleeping restfully, and have more accidents.

Addictive obsession is the inability to stop thinking about drinking and using. Some of us are obsessed with its positive effects. The obsession is based on the belief that since chemical use did wonderful things for us in the past (euphoric recall), it will probably do wonderful things for us in the future (positive expectancy). We recovering people often spend large amounts of time thinking about how good chemical use was (the good old days), and how awful it is that we can no longer experience those benefits in the future (the dreary days of recovery).

Others of us are obsessed with the negative aspects of our alcohol and other drug use. We remember all of the pain and problems caused by our addiction. We are aware that in the future we will have to deal with these problems, and we feel unprepared to do so. We look back on the past with shame, guilt, and remorse. We look ahead to the future with a sense of dread, and the belief that we won't be able to cope with what the future offers. We feel ashamed of ourselves, and believe that we will have difficulty facing other people in the world.

But now the euphoric recall kicks in. We know that in the past, when we have felt this way, a couple of drinks or a couple of hits on a joint or a couple of pills made those feelings go away. The euphoric recall invites us to believe that relief is just a swallow away. We come to believe that by using chemicals, we can make the shame, the guilt, and the remorse go away. We become obsessed with seeking this magical source of relief.

Either way, the positive expectancy causes us to believe that alcohol and other drugs will magically make us better. When positive expectancy is based on euphoric recall, we believe that we can recreate the good old days. When it is based on catastrophic recall, we believe we can escape the shame, the guilt, the remorse, and the responsibility to repair the damage we have done to ourselves simply by returning to alcohol and other drug use. In both cases, the stage is set for *compulsion.*

Unlike obsession, which is a thinking process, compulsion is a feeling process that occurs in the gut. Compulsion is a strong irrational desire to do something that we know is not in our best interest. Addictive compulsion is the irrational urge or desire to use alcohol or drugs, even though we know that the use will be harmful to us. A compulsion is not rational or logical; it simply is.

If the compulsion is strong and persists for a long time, our brain chemistry can change and a craving can be triggered. *Craving* is a body or tissue hunger for alcohol or drugs. Our brain chemistry is changed, and our body actually begins to crave chemicals. During a craving, many of us experience physical discomfort that is similar to the withdrawal we experienced shortly after we stopped using. During episodes of craving, we often experience very vivid dreams or nightmares that we have returned to drinking or other chemical use.

Addictive preoccupation makes it difficult or impossible for us to think accurately about our recovery. It must be stopped before we can make progress.

The best way to do this is to begin telling your story at Twelve Step meetings. Another way is to go to a chemical dependency counselor and have your alcohol and other drug use history taken. For yourself, reconstruct in detail the story of your alcohol and drug use. Take the memories of the "good old days" and analyze them. Get a journal and write out the story. Then take a look at each piece of the story and decide which parts were good and which ones were bad for you. When most of us do this, we find the only "good" thing was that the booze and drugs made us high and caused us to block out our awareness of how dysfunctional our lives really were.

But once our euphoric recall is challenged, the obsession quiets. When our obsession lessens, our compulsion to use alcohol or other drugs declines with it. Our addictive preoccupation is broken, and we can no longer deny reality.

Learning Nonaddictive Ways of Managing Stress

We now have to face the painful realities of our lives. During stabilization, most of us have serious problems with our spouse, family, friends, or job. Our awareness of these problems creates stress, and we must learn to manage it.

To pass through this stage of our recovery successfully, we must learn nonaddictive problem-solving strategies. We often learn these strategies from being around others and watching what they do. When we are with someone long enough, we begin to do what they are doing without thinking about it. An A.A. member once put it this way: "If you bring your body to enough meetings and spend time with enough sober drunks, the program wears off on you."

Most of us don't know how to solve problems during this time. For years, our approach has been to take a drink or a drug and think things over. Alcohol and other drugs was our all-purpose problem solver. It is important to learn new ways of solving problems. The most helpful problem solving strategy I have found asks us to solve a problem in seven stages.

1. **Problem identification.** At the first sign of a problem, stop and say to yourself, *I have a problem, and I need to do something about it.* Then take a deep breath and ask yourself, *What's really going on right now?* Formulate a response in your mind. You'll probably come up with a general statement like, *My job's lousy* or *I can't handle my spouse.* This is a good start. If you know something is wrong but can't put the problem in words, it is helpful to ask yourself questions about the key areas of your life, such as: *What is bothering me about myself right now? What is bothering me about my spouse or family right now? What is bothering me about my job right now? What is bothering me about my recovery program right now?*

2. **Problem clarification.** The next step is to figure out exactly what the problem is. It won't be helpful to be general or vague at this stage; you have to be concrete and specific. Ask yourself, *Exactly what is going on right now that I'm having difficulty handling? Who is involved?* Write down the specifics. *Where am I when this problem occurs?* Pretend you're a newspaper reporter and ask the questions — WHO, WHAT, WHEN, WHERE, WHY, and HOW. Some typical questions are: *What exactly am I or other people doing that makes it a problem? When does this happen? Where am I when it happens? Why am I experiencing this as a problem? How am I interpreting the situation that makes it more stressful than it really is?*

   It is also helpful to ask a series of questions about different areas of your life that are affected by this problem, such as: *How am I affected? How is my spouse and family affected? How is my job affected?*

   Trying to answer the questions in your head can lead to confusion. Many people find it helpful to write out their answers; this way, it is much easier to see exactly what is going on. One person I worked with said, "I hate writing this stuff down, but it does force me to sort out my head. When I think about it, I get confused and shift endlessly from one thing to another. When I write it down, I force myself to figure out exactly what is wrong."

While you are clarifying your problems, it's important to talk with other people. If we knew what the problem was, we'd be able to deal with it. Ninety percent of the problem-solving process is knowing exactly what is wrong. We can't do that by ourselves because we lack objectivity. We need help.

3. **Identifying alternatives.** The next step is to determine different ways the problem can be addressed. If you believe there is only one possible way to solve a problem, you may be locked into an irrational way of thinking. Most problems have more than one solution, but our addictive thinking keeps us from seeing other options. If you believe there is one and *only* one way to solve a problem, you probably need the help of someone else to give you a better perspective. I generally recommend that people not take action to solve the problem until they can see at least three different ways to approach it.

The Serenity Prayer tells us there are two types of problems: those that we have the power to do something about, and those that we don't. It's important to know the difference.

> *God grant me the serenity*
> *To accept the things I cannot change,*
> *The courage to change the things I can,*
> *And the wisdom to know the difference.*

There are some problems that we just cannot solve. There's very little I can do about the weather, our country's relationship with the Soviet Union, or the fact that there's a forest fire in a distant state. My solution to these problems is to adjust my attitude toward them and accept that there is nothing I can do. In A.A. terminology, I need to turn those problems over to my Higher Power. If we spend most of our time trying to solve problems that are impossible to solve, we will not have the energy to solve problems that we are capable of solving.

The other type of problem involves things I do have the ability to do something about. I can balance my checkbook, go to work, communicate with my spouse, or get up out of an easy chair and go to a meeting, even if I don't want to. These are problems that I can and need to solve. In A.A., it is called "doing the legwork." There are certain things in recovery that must be done, and most often I am the one who has to do them.

4. **Examine the alternatives.** A sign on the wall of many recovery houses advises us to "THINK, THINK, THINK." What is it we're being asked to think about? We need to think about the consequences of our behavior. We live in a world that is governed by the law of consequences. For every action, there is a reaction. It is possible to accurately predict the consequences of our actions most of the time. But developing this kind of good judgment requires practice. The exercise I recommend is to take each action and answer three questions: If I take this action, what is . . .

   - the best thing that could happen?
   - the worst thing that could happen?
   - the most likely thing that will happen?

   Remember this formula; it's important. What is the best, the worst, and the most likely thing that will happen if you attempt a specific response to a problem?

5. **Decision.** Decide what you are going to do. It is important to make a decision to do something different, to move ahead with your recovery.

6. **Action.** Once you decide what to do, you have to do it. I used to have a poster hanging in my office that reads as follows:

There are many bleached bones on the
    battlefield of decision,
Because at the moment of decision
    people pause
And die in the waiting.

Many people in A.A. say: Easy Does It But Do It. Pray for Potatoes But Pick up a Hoe. Turn It Over But Do the Legwork.

Psychologists often talk of the term "magical thinking." A person who uses "magical thinking" believes that things can be made better without doing the steps that are necessary to make them better. Earnie Larsen in his book *Stage II Recovery* states it simply and clearly when he writes, "If nothing changes, nothing changes."[4]

Magical thinking is dangerous for recovering people. The only cure for magical thinking is constructive action.

7. **Evaluation.** After you act, it is important to evaluate what happened. There is always an outcome. What we do works or it doesn't. Things get better, stay the same, or get worse. The important thing is to try and learn from the consequences. We are all fallible human beings. No matter how carefully we try to solve problems, we sometimes fail. Thomas Edison failed countless times before he found the right way to make a light bulb.

---

4. Earnie Larsen, *Stage II Recovery: Life Beyond Addiction* (San Francisco: Harper & Row, 1985).

The evaluation period is essential, but remember if your action doesn't correct the problem, you are not a failure. You have learned something—that what you tried didn't work. If something doesn't work, try something else the next time. Many people simply recycle solutions that don't work. The evaluation process answers the question, "Did it work or do I need to seek out another solution to the problem?"

Short-Term Social Stabilization

Now that we have learned how to solve problems, it's time to put that knowledge to work in a very practical way. For most of us, our addiction was destructive. We were damaged physically, psychologically, socially, and spiritually. At this stage, our physical health is probably improving, but many of us are still subject to fatigue and exaggerated reactions to stress. We may still be angry, depressed, anxious, suspicious of others, unable to trust. For many of us, our marriages are a mess, our jobs are in trouble, and our social circles have become alcohol- and drug-centered. We have few sober friends.

To stabilize, we need to take measures to hold our current life together. It's difficult to move ahead with recovery while our job is in jeopardy, we are on the verge of divorce, we're about to be arrested, or we're about to go broke or bankrupt. Short-term social stabilization means that we learn to put a bandage on the major problems of life. In A.A. language, we turn them over. We may not be able to fix them completely, but we can take action to assure that catastrophic consequences do not occur.

Cindy, a recovering cocaine addict, and her husband, John, are good examples of short-term social stabilization in action. When Cindy finally came into treatment, she and her husband were on the verge of divorce. John told Cindy that he was going to divorce her because he wasn't willing to live with her addiction any longer. This threat motivated Cindy to get into treatment. To free her up to think about her recovery, Cindy had to temporarily stabilize her marriage. In counseling, she began to recognize the effect of her addiction on John. In a couples session, Cindy and John negotiated a six-month trial period: John agreed not to divorce Cindy for a minimum of six months while she worked on her treatment. He agreed to become involved with her in counseling and to attend Al-Anon. This allowed Cindy the peace of mind of knowing she was not going to suddenly be divorced in her early recovery.

Cindy was also in debt after her cocaine addiction. She had borrowed money and had reached the limit on all of her credit cards. She and John had to put together a financial survival plan to assure that they had the resources to pay their bills, to meet daily living expenses, and to participate in necessary treatment and counseling. This, too, was part of the short-term stabilization plan.

Short-term socialization can be viewed as creating a little island of sanity in your life.

Cindy was socially isolated. She had no friends except for those who used cocaine or drank heavily. She knew she could not be around those people and stay sober, but she had no other friends. A major part of her short-term social stabilization was making a commitment to attend two Alcoholics Anonymous meetings a week and three Cocaine Anonymous meetings a week. Here, she had an opportunity to develop immediate friendships with other people who understood the problems that she was experiencing.

Short-term stabilization can be viewed as creating a little island of sanity in your life. Even though everything may be going wrong, you need a stable base from which to plan your recovery. Taking small steps to create this little clearing of sanity is essential in order to start the internal change that is necessary to bring about long-lasting changes in your life.

Development of Hope and Motivation

As we become more stable, a new feeling of hope and motivation begins to emerge. We begin to think more clearly and rationally and our emotions settle down. We begin building a new history in recovery, one day at a time. We begin seeing other people recover and progress. We become involved with a group of people who are working each day to improve their lives and health. We see that acute withdrawal and post-acute withdrawal are manageable. We come to believe that things do get better if we follow certain basic principles. The obession, compulsion, and craving to use alcohol and drugs is often diminished. We begin to believe that recovery is possible.

We find ourselves getting curious about our addiction. What is it? What caused it? What can I do to increase the quality of sobriety? We also realize there's a lot of unfinished business about our drinking and using that needs to be re-solved. These are indicators that we are now ready to start the stage I call Early Recovery.

PART IV

Early Recovery — Understanding and Acceptance

The major goal of early recovery is to change the attitudes and beliefs about alcohol and other drug use that set us up to relapse. We change our understanding of addiction and the role it plays in our lives. We explore the meaning and purpose of chemical use and learn to cope with life without it.

The Drinking Problem and the Thinking Problem

As we learned before, A.A. members like to say that alcoholism is a combination of two problems — the drinking problem and the thinking problem. The *drinking problem* refers to the alcohol and other drug use and the damage it caused to our minds and bodies. The *thinking problem* refers to the irrational thoughts, unmanageable feelings, and resulting self-defeating behaviors that accompany the drinking and using. In early recovery, the focus is on correcting the thinking problems that are associated with our addiction.

Addiction is a combination of two problems:
1. *The drinking problem — the problem with alcohol and other drug use.*
2. *The thinking problem — the problem with irrational thoughts, unmanageable feelings, and self-defeating behaviors.*

Earlier, we showed how most recovering people complete the First Step in two different ways. First, they complete the Step on an unconscious level. There is a shift in feeling, a change in emotion, a subtle, almost indescribable alteration in what we believe and do. Something is different and we know it. A "conversion" has occurred, but we cannot adequately explain it in words either to ourselves or to other people. This conversion, the unconscious process of taking the First Step, is essential. But it is not enough to produce full recovery.

The next thing we need to do is to actively work the Steps with full awareness. In actively practicing the Steps, we become aware of the actions that create the change. We learn exactly what we need to do to maintain that change. I often call the process *demystification*. At first, when we take the First Step and accept our powerlessness over alcohol or other drugs, it seems like an incomprehensible miracle. We know it has happened, but we don't understand how we did it. We aren't sure what to do to keep it. We're afraid that the miracle will undo itself.

In early recovery, we demystify the miracle by learning about the recovery process. We begin to *consciously* understand our addiction, and learn what is required from us if we are to stay in recovery. In other words, we learn the words and concepts necessary to understand what has happened to us and what we need to do to maintain the positive changes. By the end of early recovery, we are able to explain the recovery process to others.

Recovery requires two kinds of change:

1. *Unconscious* — a subtle shift in feeling and belief that motivates us to change what we do.
2. *Conscious* — an understanding of the laws and principles that create and maintain the change.

Understanding Addiction

The first task in early recovery is to develop a thorough understanding of chemical dependency or addiction. This task is intellectual, but it stirs up a lot of feelings. Recognition involves understanding addiction as a disease, applying that information to ourselves, and deciding that we do in fact have this illness, and this illness has consequences. Our recognition is not complete until we are able to defend our belief to people who might try to convince us that we are not addicted.

If you want to see how well you understand your addiction, try a simple experiment. Sit back quietly, take a deep breath, and relax. When you are in a relaxed state, say clearly to yourself: *My name is* _____ *and I am addicted to alcohol and other drugs.* Notice your response to that statement. Say it again: *My name is* _____ *and I am chemically dependent.* Some people notice that an internal argument begins. One side of them begins to say *No I'm not. I may have a drinking or drug problem, but I'm not really addicted. I'm not as bad as a heroin addict or skid-row bum. Of course I'm chemically dependent, but not in the same way as those other down-and-outers I see at meetings.*

The goal of recovery is to put the sober self back in charge.

The part of us that doubts or minimizes our addiction is called the *addictive self*. It is the habitual way of talking to ourselves that has developed to support and defend our addictive disease. The addictive self is the guardian of denial and rationalization. It is the addictive self that keeps us from clearly understanding and recognizing what chemical dependency is, the fact that we have it, and the consequences that our chemical dependency has caused in our lives.

Every addict has two distinct sides:

- the addictive self, and
- the sober self.

The goal of recovery is to put the sober self back in charge.

The goal of early recovery is to thoroughly defeat the voice of our addictive self. And this voice must be defeated through truth. We must learn the arguments necessary to undo the irrational denial system which will lead us back to drinking and using.

I often ask recovering people to have a conversation between their addictive self and their sober self. This can be done in group therapy, individual therapy, or can be written out on a sheet of paper. The process goes like this:

First, think about what you were like when you were drinking or using other drugs. Then think about the part of you in sobriety that keeps setting yourself up to get drunk or to use another drug. This is your addictive self. Just because you stop using chemicals doesn't mean that it goes away. It may go to sleep for a little while, but it can be awakened at any time to cause problems in your sobriety.

Take a sheet of paper and divide it into three sections as shown on the next page:

My description of the addictive self:

_____

_____

_____

_____

_____

- -

My addictive self . . .

1. _____
2. _____
3. _____
4. _____
5. _____
6. _____
7. _____
8. _____
9. _____
10. _____

- -

When I think about my addictive self, I feel . . .

1. _____
2. _____
3. _____
4. _____
5. _____
6. _____
7. _____
8. _____
9. _____
10. _____

In the first section, describe what your addictive self is like. One person named Jack wrote this: "My addictive self is the mean, angry, and demanding side of me when I am sober. It is the fun-loving side of me when I am drinking."

Then finish the partial sentence: "My addictive self . . . " as fast as you can at least ten times to see what comes out. Jack wrote this:

My addictive self . . .

1. is mean.
2. is angry.
3. is lonely.
4. is greedy.
5. hates for me to succeed.
6. always wants the easy way out.
7. is interested in short-term kicks regardless of the price.
8. is willing to kill me to get what it wants.
9. doesn't care about anyone or anything except getting more booze and drugs.
10. is angry when I get sober and try to stay that way.

Now in the next section, complete the partial sentence, "When I think about my addictive self, I feel . . . " ten times as fast as you can. Jack wrote this:

When I think about my addictive self I feel . . .

1. angry.
2. sad.
3. upset.
4. tight.
5. like a failure.
6. guilty.
7. dumb.
8. ashamed.
9. angry that I could be so dumb.
10. relieved I don't have to drink or use anymore.

Now take another sheet of paper and divide it into three sections, as shown on the next page:

My description of the sober self:

_____
_____
_____
_____
_____

My sober self is . . .

1. _____
2. _____
3. _____
4. _____
5. _____
6. _____
7. _____
8. _____
9. _____
10. _____

When I think about my sober self, I feel . . .

1. _____
2. _____
3. _____
4. _____
5. _____
6. _____
7. _____
8. _____
9. _____
10. _____

Think about what you are like when you are comfortable with your sobriety and write a description of the sober self in the top section of your paper. Jack wrote this: "I am interested in other people. I take good care of myself. I can handle stress well, and I cope with problems. I am connected with other people, and I feel connected with a source of strength that I choose to call God."

Now go to the partial sentence "My sober self is . . ." and finish the statement as fast as you can at least ten times. Jack wrote this: My sober self is . . .

1. intelligent.
2. warm.
3. caring.
4. sober.
5. in touch with God.
6. strong at times.
7. comfortable with my faults and weaknesses.
8. able to ask for help.
9. willing and able to help others.
10. involved with other people.

Now go to the partial sentence: "When I think about my sober self, I feel. . ." and fill in your answers. Jack wrote this: When I think about my sober self I feel . . .

1. warm.
2. caring.
3. comfortable.
4. guilty — I should have been like this all along.
5. insecure — I'm not sure I can be like this all the time.
6. tired.
7. I don't know how I feel.
8. angry.
9. this is stupid.
10. why can't I feel good about my sober self?

What happened to Jack is very common. We feel bad about our addictive self, and we know it. But somehow we can't feel good about our sober self. At this point, Jack formally introduced his sober self to his addictive self and had a long conversation. It started with his sober self asking his addictive self, "Why can't you let me feel good about being sober?" The dialogue started like this:

Sober Self:	Why can't you let me be comfortable while sober?
Addictive Self:	Because I don't want you to be sober. I need you to be drunk!
Sober Self:	Why do you need me to be drunk?
Addictive Self:	Because you are a loser and will never be able to make it without drinking and drugging. It's the only way a loser like you can feel good about yourself!
Sober Self:	That's not true. I can feel good about myself sober.
Addictive Self:	Why bother? It's easier just to drink or use drugs to feel good.
Sober Self:	I can't drink because it will kill me.
Addictive Self:	I will just make you so miserable that you'll have to drink or go crazy. I have the power to do that, so why try?

It's important to become consciously aware of what your sober and addictive selves are saying to each other. Most recovering people have regular conversations similar to the one above. Sometimes the addictive self takes over. We get into addictive thinking without even realizing it. Once you learn to tell the difference between your sober self and your addictive self, you can stop and ask yourself the question: *Who is talking right now — my sober self or my addictive self?* A sign that you have come to terms with both your addictive and sober selves is your ability to write a description of your sober self without an internal argument. After working out the dialogue between his addictive and sober selves, Jack was able to complete the description of the sober self as follows:

When I think about my sober self I feel . . .

1. secure.
2. confident.
3. warm.
4. strong.
5. at times scared, but it's nothing I can't handle.
6. alive.
7. free.
8. able to give to others.
9. responsible and mature.
10. like a sober adult.

Understanding the Role Addiction Played in Your Life

Our addictive self forced us to change physically, psychologically, socially, and spiritually. The Big Book calls it "cunning, baffling, and powerful." Our addictive self conned us into believing things that weren't true. We believed our addictive self was a friend, when it was really an enemy. We believed we could trust our addictive self to help us, when it was actually destroying us. We thought our addictive self could solve problems, when all it really did was create problems. We thought our addictive self knew how we could manage stress, when instead we became stressed to the point of collapse. We need to straighten out our thinking and see our addictive self for what it is.

Over the years, professionals have developed procedures that can help us understand our addiction. Most treatment centers use the procedures to help clients become aware of the role addiction has played in their lives. If you have not completed the following exercises, even if you have been sober for some time, I think you will find it helpful to do them. As you complete each of these exercises, be aware of the dialogue between the sober self and the addictive self. These exercises almost always start our addictive self and our sober self fighting with each other.

Reconstructing Your Life History

Remember this: Chemical dependency operates within the context of your lifestyle. To understand how your chemical dependency has progressed, it is important to understand your life.

Exercise 1: Take the time to write out an abbreviated story of your life. This history should not take more than ten to fifteen pages. A simple way to do this is to complete the tasks that follow. Discuss what you've done in this exercise at A.A. meetings, with your therapist, or with your sponsor. Write a summary of their comments and reactions.

Childhood

Task: Describe your childhood. What were your mother and father like before you were ten? Also describe each of your brothers and sisters, and how you remember them before you were ten.

How did your family affect your ability to live a happy and productive life as an adult?

Elementary School

Task: What was elementary school like for you? Did the people you meet confirm the beliefs you learned in your family, or did they show you a different way of life? How did elementary school affect your ability to live a meaningful and happy life as an adult?

Middle School and High School

Task: Describe your middle and high school experience and how this affected your ability to live a meaningful and productive life as an adult. Be sure to describe your best friends and what you learned from peers.

College/Technical School

Task: Describe what attending college or technical school was like (if you did). In what ways, if any, did that experience contribute to your ability to live a meaningful and productive life as an adult? Were there ways it was a barrier?

Military

Task: If you were in the military, what were those experiences like? Were you in combat? In what way, if any, did your military experiences contribute to your ability to live an effective life as an adult? Were there ways they were a barrier?

Work History

Task: Describe your work history. Do you consider yourself successful or unsuccessful in your ability to be productive and earn a living?

Adult Family History

Task: Describe how your adult relationships with your parents and other siblings have developed.

Adult Social History

Task: Describe how your friendships developed over the course of your life. Do you have friendships that are meaningful and comfortable?

Intimate or Marital History

Task: Describe your romantic, sexual, or marital relationships. Did you develop long-term, meaningful, and comfortable intimate relationships?

The Alcohol and Drug Use History

Exercise 2: Write down the progression of your alcohol and drug use from the time when you first started. Think about any major changes in the way you used. Note any periods when you began to use more or less. What problems were the result of your alcohol and drug use? It is helpful to divide your life into periods that range from one to five years. Be sure to list all periods when you were totally abstinent and why.

Compare Your Life History and Your Alcohol and Drug Use History

Take a sheet of paper and draw a line down the center. Label the left-hand column *Major Life Events.* Label the right-hand column *My Alcohol and Drug Use Pattern.*

In the left-hand column, list the major events in your life. It is helpful to think of your life as unfolding in chapters of a book. You may have chapters for childhood, elementary school, middle and high school, first work experience, and so forth. Another way to think about it is to identify major decisions or major changes in your life. Where did you stand at forks in the road when you had to make a decision? When did circumstances force you to an action that shaped or changed the course of your life? Be sure to identify at least six to ten such events or phases in your life.

Across from the life event, describe what your alcohol and drug use was like during that time. Be sure to note what and how much you were using. The key questions are: how much, what kind, how often, and what consequence? If family members' drug use had an impact on any period of your childhood, include that also.

This exercise will help you come to an understanding of the impact your alcohol and drug use has had on your life. You might find the exercise more difficult than it sounds. Most chemically dependent people develop a denial or rationalization system that keeps them from thinking about this. The reason for this is quite simple. If we saw the relationship of our chemical use to the course of our lives honestly and accurately, we would have to recognize how destructive it has been. And if we saw how destructive it has been, the logical thing would be to stop using. Here's an example of what your sheet might look like:

Major Life Events:	**My Alcohol and Drug Use Pattern:**
Childhood (age 0-5): Lived with parents.	Father drank heavily. Mother didn't drink at all.
Elementary school (age 6-11): I got average grades, but felt I didn't fit in and no one liked me.	Father's drinking out of control. Older sister had emotional problems caused by Dad's drinking. I would occasionally sip my Dad's beer. Felt very grown up when I did it.
Middle and high school (age 12-18): Average grades. A loner for first three years. Had many friends the last year.	No drinking first three years. Joined a gang in senior year and started drinking on Friday and Saturday nights and occasionally smoked marijuana. Felt wonderful when drinking and smoking.
College (age 19-22): Attended four years to avoid the draft. Joined fraternity. Average grades. Had a lot of fun.	Drank heavily, at times daily. Used marijuana daily and experimented with LSD and amphetamines. NO problems. Could stop when I wanted to.
Military (age 23-24): Two tours in Vietnam. Lots of combat. Lots of scars.	Never drank or drugged in the field. Got blasted on all leaves. Had blackouts and often got into fights.

The lost years (age 25-27):
Home from Vietnam. Few friends. Felt like I was going crazy and no one understood me.

I drank and drugged daily. I blamed it all on my Vietnam experiences.

Marriage (age 28-31):
Met and fell in love with Ruth. Married in six months. First steady job as a store manager. Two children in two years. My family was the most important thing in my life.

Ruth changed my life. I cut back on drinking. Stopped drugs completely. Did well for a year. Felt great pressure being a parent; drank heavily. When drinking I did things to wife and kids that I regretted later.

Chemical dependency treatment (age 31):

I went into treatment as a result of my wife threatening to divorce me and my boss threatening to fire me.

Finding the Purpose Alcohol and Drugs Served

Exercise 3: Alcohol and drug use served a purpose in our lives. We used it to accomplish something. Sometimes, we used it to exaggerate our personal strengths. At other times, we used it to overcome our weaknesses. A way to figure out some of the reasons you used alcohol and other drugs is to write down on a separate piece of paper your responses to the following questions:

1. What **strengths** did I seem to have when I was drinking (or drugging) that I don't have now that I am sober? What can I do to develop those strengths in sobriety?

2. What **weaknesses** do I have now that make me so un-comfortable I often feel like drinking? What can I do to overcome or accept those weaknesses without using alcohol or drugs?
3. What types of **problems** or unpleasant situations did I use booze and drugs to cope with or avoid? Now that I am sober, how can I cope with those situations without using?

Acceptance of Addictive Disease

Acceptance is the ability to think about what happened while we were using alcohol and other drugs without feeling pain. It is an emotional process that involves the resolution of shame, guilt, and unresolved painful experiences that occurred during addiction. Many recovering people carry these unresolved painful memories for years. Most of the time they feel fine, but when they think or talk about past drinking and drug use, the pain, shame, and guilt come back.

Many of us try to cope with those feelings by not thinking about the memories that produce them. This works in the short run, but eventually the feelings come back. These painful feelings can be resolved by working a Twelve Step program, perhaps getting involved in counseling or therapy, and learning to identify and talk about memories and the feelings they cause. When we have fully accepted our addiction, our past alcohol and drug use will no longer have the power to hurt us.

The Big Book of Alcoholics Anonymous tells us that we are going to know a new freedom and a new happiness, that we will not regret the past nor wish to shut the door upon it, that we will comprehend the word *serenity* and we will know peace. In spite of our past history and all the pain and problems we have caused to ourselves and others, we can know serenity and peace of mind.

To resolve our painful memories, it is helpful to understand why we still have them and how we maintain them in sobriety.

We keep our memories unresolved when we have painful or traumatic experiences and refuse to talk about them later. The worse the trauma, the more unresolved pain. Most of us experienced pain or trauma while we were either intoxicated or in withdrawal, but we often dismiss these as meaningless. *After all,* we say to ourselves, *I was drunk at the time and drunks can't feel any pain. Why worry about it now that I'm sober?*

What happened to us then does have long-term emotional consequences. The pain and trauma is recorded in the unconscious mind. Later, something can trigger the memory and the painful feelings come back. This is called a flashback. This is the way the unconscious mind gets us to think and talk about the memory so we can resolve it.

The painful memory is maintained by trying to dismiss it from our minds whenever it intrudes. This works for a little while, but the memory and feelings will come back again. We get in the habit of blocking out memories that carry painful feelings. We can get so good at it that we do it without thinking. Unfortunately, this doesn't make it go away for good. The memory will return again and again until we think and talk about it. Here is the story of Jack:

> There was an evening where I decided to see what it was like to "go beyond drunk." I consumed a fifth of bourbon over a period of three and one-half hours. As I was drinking down the last few gulps, my head was spinning and I was so dizzy I could barely lift the bottle. I chugged down the last couple of drinks, and then I threw up all over myself and the recreation room I was in. A few moments later, I remember being placed on a couch. I was lying there as if asleep with my hands crossed on my chest. There were people standing around the couch yelling at me and trying to talk with me. I was not responding. They criticized me

for being so drunk that I couldn't move. I said to myself, *I can move, I'll show them.* And I tried to open my eyes, but I couldn't. I tried to say something, but I couldn't. I tried to move my arms and legs, but I couldn't. I panicked. I felt like I was going to die, but I couldn't move. One by one, I heard the people walk away and leave me alone. I tried desperately to scream out for help, but I couldn't.

This was very traumatic, so traumatic that he pushed it from memory for many years into sobriety. But the memory kept intruding. He couldn't sleep on his back without feeling a strange sense of panic. When people yelled at him, he felt like he was suffocating. The memory that caused this had tried to surface, but he wouldn't let it. He kept pushing it from his mind. One night while he was telling his story at an A.A. meeting, the memory returned. As he tried to talk about it he started to cry. He felt panicky, abandoned, and like he was going to die. When he stopped talking he felt better. He didn't know why; he just did. After the meeting, he talked about this with his sponsor and then at several other meetings. People listened and understood because they had similar experiences. With time and discussion, the power this memory had to hurt him went away. Today, he can think and talk about that incident without feeling any pain. As a matter of fact, he can laugh at it.

One woman, Joanne, had many blackouts during her drinking career. When she got sober, she had nightmares of being trapped and of people touching and pushing her. As she reconstructed her drinking history, she remembered being sexually abused when she was too drunk to fight back. At first, the memories were painful and fragmented, and she pushed them out of her mind. But with the help of a counselor she was able to remember what happened. Although the feelings of pain, helplessness, and betrayal were intense, each time she talked about the incident the pain was less. One night she talked about it at an A.A. meeting. Several women in the group had similar experiences, but were afraid to think or talk about them. They got together after the meeting and, by talking to each other about them, the memories, over time, lost their power to hurt so much.

When we experience trauma, adrenaline floods our system, causing rapid heartbeat, shortness of breath, and severe muscle tension. If the trauma is bad enough, we go into shock. If it is intolerable, we black out, unaware of what is happening. In shock, we are unable to feel physical and emotional effects of the trauma. We have shut down to protect our nervous system from becoming overloaded. We become numb and dazed. There is often a vacant or distant stare in our eyes. If we are drunk or high at the time, other people can mistake our shock for our intoxication.

This is followed by a "rebound" stage. The person begins to feel restored to the preshock state. The body begins to rebalance and the emotions that were shut down begin to surface. Now the person has a desire and a need to talk. If the event is talked out, it can be resolved. If it is blocked out, it will come back.

Many of us feel intense shame and guilt when the rebound stage begins. We may believe the traumatic event was our fault, or feel that if we had not been drinking or drugging that it would not have happened. We experience shame. We feel that we must be defective because of what happened, and we are afraid or unwilling to talk with anyone about this. We often begin drinking or using drugs to get rid of these unresolved painful feelings.

How do you know if you have unresolved, repressed traumatic experiences from your chemical use? Your answers to the following questions can help you decide. Circle the answer that best describes your situation.

1. Are there periods of time, when you know you were drinking and drugging, but you cannot remember what happened?   YES   NO
2. Are you able to remember terrible things that happened while you were using, but don't believe they affected you?   YES   NO
3. When you are thinking about or talking about your alcohol or other drug use history, do you
   - A. become overly emotional?   YES   NO
   - B. become emotionally numb?   YES   NO
   - C. become unable to concentrate or pay attention?   YES   NO
   - D. become confused or unable to think clearly?   YES   NO
   - E. have intrusive, fragmented memories?   YES   NO
   - F. feel helpless and hopeless?   YES   NO
   - G. feel painful physical sensations or extreme tension?   YES   NO

If you circled yes four or more times, you probably have unresolved memories related to your alcohol and drug use. You could probably benefit from talking it through with your sponsor, at meetings, or with a counselor.

At the beginning of early recovery, you may feel helpless about what you did while you were using. You probably feel helpless because you believe there is nothing you can do about the past and there is no way to make the pain go away. This isn't true. There is a way to resolve the pain associated with these memories. A number of principles can guide you.

Resolving the Pain of Addiction Experiences

All chemically dependent people have painful memories. There is nothing wrong with this. It is a natural consequence of having the disease of addiction. In sobriety, these painful memories will periodically come back and make us feel un-comfortable. This is "a need to resolve." It is natural and normal for this to happen.

We need to think and talk about these experiences to re-solve our pain about them. If we simply push them out of our mind, they will come back later.

We don't need to do it alone. Most people are unable to think their way through this unresolved pain because their unconscious mind is protecting them.

If we are in a dangerous or unsupportive environment when the need to resolve emerges, we don't have to think or talk about the memories until it is appropriate to do so.When a painful memory surfaces, it is important to get to a safe environment, where there are people who will listen to us, understand what we're saying, take us seriously, and affirm that the experience was real and important. Most A.A. meet-ings are safe places. So are most support groups or private therapy sessions.

Once in a safe environment, it is important to describe our memories to others as clearly and accurately as possible. As we begin discussing the experience, we will cycle in and out of vivid memories and painful feelings. Our emotions may shut down; we may overreact; we may even experience intense visual images and body sensations that are similar to what we experienced at the time.

You have already lived through the memory and survived. The memory does not have the power to physically hurt or kill you. Reexperiencing the feelings will be uncomfortable but, if done in a safe environment, will not seriously hurt you.

Each time we talk through the memory, we will experience less pain and tension. Eventually, we will experience a sense of relief and be able to think about the memory without feeling any pain. We will become free of the memory.

There are four ways to resolve the pain of our memories. These are

- listening to the stories of others,
- telling our story,
- participating in counseling, and
- working the Twelve Step program, particularly Steps Four through Seven.

Let's look at each of these.

Listening to the Stories of Others

At meetings, we hear other people tell the story of their alcohol and drug use. By listening to someone else's story, we begin to see ourselves in the experiences of others. We see that we are not unique. We see that we do belong. If we have pushed painful memories from our minds, they return as we listen to others tell their stories. We can take note of our painful memories and begin to talk them through with others.

Telling Our Story

One of the most powerful ways to remember and resolve the pain from the past is to tell our story at meetings. Most of us are nervous and apprehensive before we start. We might prepare an outline of what we're going to say. We stand in front of the group and begin to speak. Then something magical happens. We forget the outline as memories begin to flood into our minds. We begin to say what we need to say instead of what we planned to say. Emotions begin to well up. Many people become tearful. Others openly cry.

What is happening? We are beginning to experience the same feelings we had not allowed during our drinking and drug use. As these painful experiences emerge, an emotional catharsis is taking place. The pain is being felt and expressed. At the end, there is a sense of relief and there can be a resolution.

One person in A.A. told me that most alcoholics don't know

what their story is until they have told it at meetings at least ten times, because each time new memories emerge.

Telling your story is so vital a part of recovery that I believe it should be done at least three to five times during the first year of recovery.

Participating in Counseling

A counselor can get us ready to tell our story by helping us remember what happened during episodes of alcohol and other drug use. A skilled counselor can help us fill in memory gaps by asking us questions and using guided imagery. We use guided imagery by getting into a deeply relaxed state and letting our mind go back to a period in time shortly before the memory gap started. We are asked to remember exactly what was happening—exactly what we saw, heard, felt, and experienced. We focus on what was happening and how we felt about it. We are led step by step into the memory gap. Memories often come back that we thought were forgotten. Many of the memories can be painful. A trained counselor can help us to remember the experience and release the pain.

The combination of telling your story to a sponsor, at meetings, and to a counselor can help you recover faster.

Working the Steps

During the early recovery period, most recovering people work Steps Four through Seven of the A.A. program. These Steps deal with the internal change process.

The Twelve Step Program in Early Recovery

Since it is important that all recovering people understand the Twelve Steps and the principles that underlie them, we will review these Steps in detail.

Step 4: Made a searching and fearless moral inventory of ourselves.

The key concept here is the word *moral*. What does it mean to be moral? Morality concerns itself with right and wrong behavior. In order to determine right and wrong behavior, we need to decide on a standard. What is the standard or yardstick against which we judge our behavior right and wrong?

In judging my own behavior as right or wrong, I use the standard of life, both my own and others.' Anything that promotes a full and abundant life is good. Anything that destroys or encumbers life is bad. I view life as a biopsychosocial and spiritual process, and to me, anything that damages or destroys physical, psychological, social, and spiritual life and health is bad. Anything that enhances these areas is good. I believe we were born to live as fully as possible. Recovery means learning to live again. Any behavior that moves us from full health and vitality into sickness of mind, body, and spirit is wrong. Any behavior that moves us from sickness and near death to full health and vitality is good.

The good life (healthy behavior) is based on interdependence with other people, but we recognize that it is in nobody's best interest to infringe on the rights of others, or to hurt others. We try to seek out situations in life that are win-win. Win-win situations are those where everyone benefits. There are no losers. People who move toward the healthy life, toward the good, realize that there are laws that govern the universe.

- Physical laws determine how to stay healthy.
- Psychological laws determine how we can use our minds properly.
- Social laws dictate the effectiveness of our relationships.
- Spiritual laws dictate how to build an effective relationship with a Higher Power.

Moral behavior is the behavior which corresponds with those laws.

I often paraphrase the Fourth Step to read, "I will evaluate my current strengths and weaknesses so I can build upon my strengths and overcome my weaknesses." A *strength* is something that allows us to live more fully over the long run of our lives. A *weakness* is something that weakens us in the long run and eventually causes us to become sick and die.

It's important to write down a Fourth Step: it's only when we confront ourselves in writing with all of our strengths and weaknesses that we can truly come to a better understanding of who we are and how we conduct our lives.

Step 5: Admitted to God, to ourselves, and to another human being the exact nature of our wrongs.

This Step is vital. We must consciously acknowledge to ourselves our strengths and our weaknesses. We must consciously affirm our human fallibility to a Higher Power. We must also share with at least one other human being the exact nature of our wrongs. Notice the phrase "exact nature of our wrongs." Step Five doesn't say we have to tell other people the gory details of every wrongdoing we have ever committed. What is important here is that we understand the general principles that underlie the behaviors that are destroying our lives.

Another way to paraphrase the Fifth Step is as follows: "I will discuss my self-evaluation with at least one other person and listen to the feedback."

Step 6: Were entirely ready to have God remove all these defects of character.

The Sixth Step has been one of the hardest for me to understand. Not until I had a long conversation with Father Martin did the Step begin to make sense. He explained to me that God can be relied on to give us courage, strength, hope, and the means to solve our problems. We must provide the action.

God works through natural means. When God created a human mind that's capable of reason, God didn't command us not to use it. When God created a universe based on the law of consequence, God didn't command us to ignore the consequences of our behavior.

The Sixth Step simply tells us to become willing to let go of our character defects and their consequences. As we become consciously aware of what our character defects are and how they're hurting us, we can then begin to change.

Remember this: Each character defect is two-sided. There is an up side and a down side. The down side consists of all the pain and disadvantages the character defect causes. The up side consists of all the pleasure and good times the character defect provides.

In psychological terms, the up side is called *secondary gain*. Every psychological problem creates pain, but it also produces benefits called secondary gains. People with grandiosity problems will alienate others and begin to feel very lonely. They will also feel powerful and better than anyone else. To overcome a character defect such as grandiosity, a person may do four things: (1) consciously recognize the character defect, (2) recognize both the benefits and disadvantages the character defect creates, (3) recognize that the disadvantages outweigh the benefits, and (4) find positive ways to get the benefits without experiencing the disadvantages.

Ed was a grandiose drunk. He believed the world stopped at the tip of his nose. He loved nothing better than to gather people around him in bars and brag. When he got sober, he brought his grandiosity right with him into recovery. His constant bragging and exaggerating started arguments and drove others away.

As a result of a Fifth and Sixth Step, Ed recognized what was happening and what was causing it to happen, and he decided to change. At first, he just stopped his grandiose behavior. "If it hurts me and my recovery it has got to go," he said. But he had nothing to replace it with. He was still lonely, and on top of it he was constantly battling the urge to monopolize conversations. His sponsor helped him to see that there was a positive side to grandiosity. He enjoyed leading and helping people, and being recognized for it. His sponsor showed him how to work with newcomers in a way that gave him all of those things. In therapy, Ed learned to balance talking with listening. He learned how to ask questions instead of telling people what to do. He learned how to share thoughts and feelings instead of forcing them on others. He kept the positive aspects of the defect while giving up the negative side.

I paraphrase Step Six to read: "I will become willing to do the work necessary to overcome these weaknesses by paying attention to the daily pain and problems that they cause." To get people to take action on this Step, I ask them to keep a daily journal documenting each time they notice themselves using a character defect that was discovered in their Fourth and Fifth Step. I then ask them to note both the positive and the negative consequences of that behavior.

Step 7: Humbly asked Him to remove our shortcomings.

Again, this Step baffled me. I know that periodically miracles do happen, but they are few and far between. They are also unreliable. I could not believe that the founders of A.A. were instructing members to simply sit around and wait for a miracle.

In talking with Father Martin, I developed an understanding that God gives us the courage, the strength, the hope, and the means to remove our character defects. We have to do the footwork. We have to take the action. It's not enough to simply pray to God and sit back and do nothing. We must pray, visualize the desired outcome, become willing to change, and then when the opportunity is provided, we must be willing to take action.

In a recent lecture, Father Martin said, "God always answers prayers, but He doesn't always answer them the way we would like Him to. If we pray that we want to become a doctor, God always answers. He says, 'Go to medical school'." This is true of all prayers. If we want to overcome irrational behavior, God says, "Go to therapy." If we want to overcome problems with our spouse, God says, "Go to marital counseling." If we want to find a better job, God says, "Go into job retraining, fill out a resume, and start to look."

By working Steps Four to Seven, we change on the inside. We get well from the inside out.

PART V

Middle Recovery — Achieving Lifestyle Balance

In Middle Recovery, we begin to repair the parts of our lives that were damaged by our addiction. We evaluate our goals, examine our lives, and make changes. It's not easy, and it requires absolute honesty, but if we persist, we can bring new meaning, purpose, and happiness into our lives.

If you got hit by a truck, the paramedics would stop the bleeding, bandage you up, and take you to the hospital for more intensive treatment. Recovery from chemical dependency works in a similar way. In transition, we get hit by the truck called addiction; in stabilization we stop the bleeding; in early recovery we bandage our lives until we can get enough recovery under our belts to make serious, long-term changes in our lives. These long-term changes are what middle recovery is about.

By the end of early recovery, most of us are regularly involved in Twelve Step meetings and possibly in therapy. We used this time to put bandages on our problems. We have done what's necessary to make sure we didn't get fired, divorced, put in jail, or go bankrupt. Our attention has been on our number one priority — not drinking today and learning the skills necessary to stay sober. We are coping on a day-to-day basis, but do not have a well balanced or highly satisfying lifestyle. Things are much better than they were during our active addiction, but there is still a great deal of work to be done.

Resolving Feelings of Letdown

It can be discouraging to look at life after six to eighteen months of sobriety and find a lot more work to be done. During early recovery, we worked hard to change our addictive thinking, destructive emotions, and self-defeating behavior. It's a letdown to learn that internal change is not the end of the recovery process, but the beginning of a fundamental lifestyle change.

Many recovering people become so discouraged they resist further growth. They attend many Twelve Step meetings, concentrate on the first three Steps, and yet resist making any real changes in their relationships or lifestyles. Instead of using the Twelve Step program to learn how to live a meaningful and productive life, they stay at an unsatisfying job, feel trapped in a bad relationship, and go to meetings to ventilate their unhappiness. This carries over into their social lives too.

During early recovery, most of our friends are recovering people, and what we have in common is the program. We're often uncomfortable with "earth people" who are not working the Twelve Step program. There are good reasons for this. In early recovery, we go to meetings to save our lives, not to make social contacts. To stay sober, we need to live and breathe the program. Most of our old friends are active addicts, and we have to stay away from them in order to stay sober. Most people who aren't addicts don't understand what we are going through, and many are codependent (those whose lives have become unmanageable as a result of living in a committed relationship with an addicted person) with no recovery program of their own. The program is an island of sanity in an addictive world, and we spend a lot of time there. As we enter middle recovery, we recognize the need to expand this island of sanity into other areas of our lives. In A.A., this is called practicing the principles "in all our affairs."

Middle recovery confronts us with a major choice. Do we begin to rebuild our lifestyle, using recovery principles, or do we try to avoid making any real changes? At this point, some people get stuck. Others move ahead. Those who get stuck stop the recovery process. They rationalize by saying, "I'm not drinking and I'm going to meetings! That's all I need to do!" Those who have the courage to move ahead are willing to confront reality. They are willing to pay the price to develop a balanced lifestyle and find meaning and purpose in sobriety.

Don't underestimate the power of this letdown. Many of us become depressed during this period of time. We feel weak and hopeless. It is a period of high relapse risk. We begin to ask the question, *Sobriety for what? Why did I stay sober all this time if I still have problems?*

John is an insurance salesman. He used to like it because he could sell enough insurance in two days to support his drinking for the next three. When he got sober, he found he wasn't happy as an insurance salesman. He didn't like the hours or the amount of time he had to spend away from his family. But after fifteen years, he was making nearly $65,000 a year and didn't know another way to earn that kind of money. In middle recovery, he realized he needed a job more suited to his sober self.

John feels overwhelmed at the thought of changing careers. Instead of talking about the problem and making plans to change, he just keeps going to meetings and ventilating his frustration and unhappiness. He uses his meetings to justify standing still, instead of using recovery principles to rebuild his life.

Abby has two years of sobriety. She is desperately unhappy with her marriage. Her husband is basically a good man, but he is not assertive. He places her at the center of his universe and will do anything to make her happy. But Abby isn't in love with her husband. There is no passion, and at times she doesn't even respect him.

Why did I marry him? she repeatedly asks herself. She doesn't like the answer. She drank heavily when they were dating. She got drunk on their wedding night and doesn't even remember if they had sex. She drank throughout their marriage. Her husband's strongest asset had been his support of her drinking. Now that she is sober, he has little to offer.

With two years of sobriety, Abby wants more out of her marriage. Her husband doesn't know how to give more, and Abby is afraid to ask. Their marriage is bandaged together. There's no major crisis, but she is unhappy and unfulfilled. She knows she needs to do something, but she's afraid to try.

Instead of getting marital counseling, Abby uses Twelve Step meetings to vent her frustration and disappointment in her marriage. She found a group of other recovering women who were unhappy in their marriages and turned to them for support. They reinforced that there is nothing she can do. "First Things First," they reminded her. "No problem is so bad that a drink won't make it worse." She took things One Day at a Time and didn't make waves. She tried not to think about what her life would be like if the marriage did not improve. She practiced Easy Does It in her marriage. She interpreted this to mean "don't do anything at all."

Abby is in a "demoralization crisis." She knows she needs to work on her marriage or get out of it, but the thought overwhelms her. It is easier for her to use her recovery program as a hideout from problems, rather than as a tool for growth and change.

To bring an end to this kind of crisis, we need a strong belief that it is possible to repair past damage and create a better life.

We must also believe that change is worth the price. This takes more than intellectual understanding. We need role models who can show us the benefits of changing our lives. Once we believe a balanced life is possible, we can choose to move ahead, or stick with the safe ground of early recovery. Now we have a choice. We are no longer victims.

Repairing the Damage

The next task in middle recovery is repairing the damage we have done through our illness. In A.A. terms, this is called "making amends." We need to make amends for one simple reason: although we are not responsible for having the disease, we are responsible for repairing the damage we have done.

An epileptic who has a seizure while driving is responsible for the damage. Heart attack victims have to pay hospital bills. Responsible people need to repair the damage caused by their disease.

In early recovery, the primary focus is on internal change. Our job is to put a bandage on our life problems so we can change our thinking, feelings, and behavior related to our addictions.

When we enter middle recovery, we find that "putting a bandage on the problem" is not enough. In middle recovery, our goal is to identify problems and resolve them.

RESOLVE is an interesting word. RE means *to do again*. SOLVE means *to find a solution*. When we resolve something, we find a solution once and for all. We stop coping with the same problem over and over again. We stop "re-solving" it. We discover the fundamental core issue and put the problem to rest for good.

How Steps Eight and Nine Can Help

The Twelve Steps tell us to start putting problems to rest by taking Steps Eight and Nine. Step Eight suggests that we make a list of all the persons we have harmed and become willing to make amends to them all. This Step clearly instructs us to get involved in the real world and become ready to fix the damage we have caused. Step Nine suggests that we make "direct amends to such people wherever possible, except when to do so would injure them or others." The mandate is clear. It is not enough to stop using chemicals and to go to meetings, if we continue to live a self-destructive lifestyle.

"Making amends" means to fix something. When we make amends, we repair our broken relationships. Step Nine is acting on the plan we created in Step Eight. We actually go and apologize to the people we have hurt. But it must be more than a verbal apology. If we have stolen something, we return it. If we have hurt someone, we attempt to make up for the pain in some tangible way. The goal is to clean up the rubble from the past so we will be free to move ahead in the future. We must be willing to make restitution.

This is difficult. We can create enough stress to cause a relapse if we attempt this too early in recovery. We must change on the inside before we are emotionally and spiritually mature enough to handle the stress of completing these Steps.

One way to work Step Eight is to take a sheet of paper and label the top Persons Who Were Harmed by My Chemical Dependency. Draw three vertical columns on the page. In the first column, write the name of the person who was harmed; in the second column, write what you did that harmed them; and in the third column, write what you will have to do to make amends. The top of your page should look like this:

Persons Who Were Harmed by My Chemical Dependency		
People Who I Harmed	What I Did that Harmed Them	What I Need to Do to Make Amends

Fill out the page as honestly and completely as you can and show it to your sponsor. You could discuss it at your Twelve Step meeting, or bring it to another therapy group.

Starting A Self-Regulated Recovery Program

As we recognize new problems, it becomes obvious that we need to make changes in our recovery programs to solve them.

John, the insurance salesman mentioned earlier, realized that he needed to change jobs. He needed job training and, to get that, he had to alter his recovery program. Instead of attending five A.A. meetings each week, he went to four and replaced one with a career counseling session.

Abby made amends to her husband, but very little changed. She was still dissatisfied with the low level of intimacy in her marriage. Abby and her husband decided to go to marriage counseling. Abby went from four meetings a week to three, and she replaced one meeting with a marriage counseling session and private time with her husband.

If we want a balanced lifestyle, we must be willing to go to any lengths to get it. Often, this can mean modifying our recovery programs to include other forms of education and therapy.

Establishing Lifestyle Balance

During early recovery, many of us live rigid lives that have little variety or balance. I call it *unidimensional living*. When we have balanced our lifestyles, we have good things going in more than one area. We have meaningful and productive jobs, a satisfying love relationship, and good relationships with family. We not only have a solid Twelve Step recovery program with a good sponsor and numerous friends in the program, we also have friends and associates who are outside the program.

86

A healthy life requires balancing the physical, psychological, social, and spiritual aspects of life. Let's look at each of these.

Physical Health in Recovery

Getting physically healthy is an important part of middle recovery. Physical health typically improves with abstinence. Unfortunately, many recovering people develop habits that undermine the benefits of abstinence. These self-defeating habits include poor diet, excessive use of cigarettes and caffeine, and improper exercise. Let's look at each of these areas.

Poor Diet

With sobriety, many recovering people begin eating more junk food such as cakes, candies, and ice cream. Many people have poor diet habits because they have an eating disorder. Proper nutrition is necessary for good health. Proper nutrition means eating three well-balanced meals and perhaps one or two small snacks a day, possibly supplemented with vitamins if needed. If you are unable to maintain a healthy diet and your self-destructive eating habits are out of control, you may have an eating disorder and require treatment. A good place to go is Overeaters Anonymous (O.A.).

Nicotine and Caffeine

It has been well-documented that smoking is harmful to your health. Bob Earll, author of *I Got Tired of Pretending* (published by Recovery Resources, Phoenix, Az.) told the story of being confronted with the seriousness of his smoking addiction. While consulting at a suicide prevention agency, he was smoking. The person he was working with said, "Bob, we believe that smoking is a form of slow suicide. Every time you smoke a cigarette, it's like putting a small, loaded gun in your mouth. Every time you inhale, it's like shooting a small bullet into your brain."

Bob was shaken up by this analogy. He was so upset that he needed a cigarette to get over the anxiety. That confrontation was the start of the process of quitting smoking and eventually he did stop.

Quitting smoking can be just as difficult for some, or even more so, as quitting drinking or other drugs. Nicotine *is* a drug and we may need the support of therapy, a recovery program, or both for this addiction as well as what we've identified as our "primary" addiction. It may be helpful to see ourselves as addicts and therefore powerless over *all* mood-altering chemicals.

A lot of recovering people radically increase the caffeine they use. Many drink as many as fifteen cups of coffee a day or more. "Why not?" they ask. "Caffeine is pretty harmless, isn't it?" The answer is no, it isn't. Fifteen cups of caffeinated coffee a day (or its equivalent in cola beverages) can create symptoms of anxiety, sleep disturbances, and agitation. These symptoms can lower the quality of recovery and even increase the risk of relapse.

Many recovering people forget that caffeine is a stimulant. In large doses, it produces symptoms similar to amphetamine and cocaine intoxication. Caffeine is addictive. At first, the mood-altering effects are pleasant. As caffeine builds, it takes more and more to get the desired effect. When a person tries to stay away from caffeine, there can be withdrawal symptoms such as headaches, fatigue, and lethargy. The symptoms may then be alleviated by more caffeine use. High tolerance can last for years. For many people, tolerance eventually decreases, and they experience the symptoms of caffeine toxicity. They can become anxious, paranoid, easily startled. They can have constant tremors in their hands, and develop insomnia or strange dreams and nightmares. Eventually, stress-related illness can develop.

While not as obviously destructive as nicotine, caffeine use can definitely lower the quality of sobriety and increase the risk of relapse. This is especially true for persons recovering from addiction to a stimulant such as cocaine or amphetamine. For them, heavy use of caffeine can trigger cravings for other stimulants.

Improper Exercise

Many recovering alcoholics have problems with exercise by doing too much, too little, or none at all. Each extreme can be dangerous. Improper eating habits (perhaps fueled by an eating disorder) can compound the problem, causing recovering alcoholics to gain weight or to lose so much weight that they feel weak. As a result, they become prone to other diseases and illnesses.

On one hand, some recovering people don't exercise at all and their physical health suffers. On the other hand, many recovering people become compulsive about exercise. They don't exercise for the positive effects on their health, but rather for the "high" that can eventually come with prolonged strenuous activity.

Compulsive running is one example. Sometimes this ordinarily healthy activity is carried to an extreme, with a runner devoting most of his or her free time to achieving higher and higher mileage. Possibly going out every day for hours, compulsive runners may feel severe discomfort or withdrawal if circumstances force them to miss a day's run. The consuming effect of an exercise compulsion can throw a person's life out of balance, so that important areas of recovery are neglected or ignored altogether.

Healthful exercise is essential, but many of us tend to do everything to excess. One recovering person put it this way: "If it feels good, I do it until I drop."

Psychological Health in Recovery

Psychologically healthy people have gotten into the habit of using their minds in healthy ways. They have learned how to think clearly, logically, and rationally. They have learned to manage their feelings and emotions. They can use good judgment and regulate their behavior. Let's look at these in more detail.

Thinking Straight

Thinking is logical when it follows rules. We start with simple thoughts and build upon them in a consistent way. One thought leads logically to the next. A good way to be sure our thinking is logical is to write out our sequence of thoughts from beginning to end to see if any of the thoughts contradict each other.

Thinking is rational when our thoughts correspond with what is happening in the world around us.

> Mary thought she was a great thinker before she got sober. "I used to think wonderful things," she told her therapy group. "The problem is nobody could understand what I was thinking. I always thought I was smarter than everybody else. Now that I'm sober I can see that the booze and the drugs were scrambling my brain. No sober person could have made sense out of my thinking because it was crazy."

Managing Feelings and Emotions

Psychologically healthy people know what they feel. They can usually put their feelings into words and tell them to others. Chemical dependency can cause brain dysfunction that distorts feelings. Sometimes, we feel too much and overreact. At other times, we feel too little and numb off. An important part of recovery is learning what we are feeling, deciding if those feelings are appropriate to the situation, and learning to express them appropriately to others. In recovery, we learn to separate appropriate feelings from overreactions.

Allen was recovering from cocaine dependency. He thought that just because he felt a certain way about something it must be true. When he got sober, he changed his mind. "I can't believe how screwed up my emotions are," he told his recovery group. "I get angry for no reason at all. Sometimes, I overreact to little things. It's like my brain multiplies every feeling times ten. Now I know that I sometimes need to put a filter between my brain and my mouth if I'm going to settle my life down."

Using Good Judgment

Judgment is the ability to predict what's going to happen as a result of what we do. People with good judgment know what's going to happen. They're rarely surprised, and when they are, the surprises seldom cause a crisis. People with bad judgment, on the other hand, are constantly surprised and generally have no idea what caused the problem. As a result, they are in constant crisis.

John, for example, didn't like to pay bills. He found it a nuisance and would put it off until the last minute. One day he came home and found his apartment was cold because his gas had been turned off. When he went to turn on a light so he could look up the number of the gas company, the lights wouldn't come on. He picked up the phone to call directory assistance, and the phone was dead. He couldn't understand why all of his utilities had been turned off. He felt outraged and complained that the utility companies were unfair.

Louise had a bad battery in her car. She knew she needed a new battery but just never got around to buying one. One night the temperature dropped to near zero and her car wouldn't start. She complained about her lousy luck for weeks after that.

No one has perfect judgment. We are all fallible human beings. The point is, we need to be willing to learn. The more we learn, the better our judgment gets.

To learn from our behavior, we must become aware of what we are doing and what happens as a result. We need to take responsibility for the outcomes of our behavior. People with poor judgment refuse to accept responsibility for the consequences they create in their lives. They don't plan. When things happen, they blame it on someone else, instead of thinking about how they could produce different outcomes. No learning occurs. They are victimized by a recurring cycle of crisis.

> Mark came into sobriety with a chip on his shoulder. The world was against him, and he knew it. The motto of his recovery was "Nothing I ever do comes out right." He blamed others for the crises in his life. Eventually, he learned that his poor judgment was the cause of many of his problems. He put it this way: "I thought my boss caused all my problems at work. I was convinced he didn't like me because I was a sober drunk. As I began talking about my work problems with my sponsor and counselor, I found out different. I was making mistakes at work that caused the problems. Even though I was sober, I used bad judgment. I was the one that had to learn how to change. Once I began connecting problems at work to my own bad decisions, I could change. Things are a lot better now."

Controlling Our Behavior

When we are in control of our behavior, we can resist self-destructive impulses and do what's in our best interest, even if we don't feel like it. Since we're not perfect, we occasionally give in to temptations or fail to act in our own best interest, but this rarely happens in areas that could have a major impact on our lives.

Some people take issue with the notion that we should control our behavior. I have been asked, "Aren't we powerless over everything? Don't we just need to turn everything over to a Higher Power?" I don't believe so. I think we need to divide our actions into those we have control over and those we don't. This is the essence of the Serenity Prayer which reads: "God grant me the serenity to accept the things I cannot change, the courage to change the things I can, and the wisdom to know the difference." If we were truly powerless over everything, the Serenity Prayer would read: "God grant me the serenity to blindly accept everything that happens to me."

The slogans — Easy Does It But Do It; Turn It Over But You Do the Legwork; and Pray for Potatoes, But Be Willing to Pick up the Hoe — more fully reflect, in my opinion, the essence of the Twelve Step approach to behavioral control. If there is something in our lives that we are legitimately unable to control, it is best to turn it over to our Higher Power and trust that it will be taken care of. We are not the keeper of the universe. It is not our responsibility to make sure that everything goes well in the world.

But we are obligated to determine what things we have the power to change and must be willing to take responsibility for doing them. This is what is meant by doing the legwork.

If we developed a strong foundation of psychological health as a child, it will be easier for us to rebuild our psychological strengths in recovery. If we were raised in a dysfunctional family, we will probably have difficulty in recovery, because the problems we developed before our addiction will tend to return, now that we are sober. (We will talk more about this in Part VI, which focuses on the late recovery period.)

Remember this: chemical addiction causes brain dysfunction, and brain dysfunction disorganizes the personality. Many of us believe that as soon as we are sober, we should be instantly psychologically healthy. The long-term brain dysfunction (post-acute withdrawal) can prevent us from being fully functional for periods of six to eighteen months into recovery. As the symptoms of brain dysfunction begin to clear up, our preaddictive personality traits return. We return to the same level of psychological health we had before we became addicted. This is why the Twelve Step program places so much emphasis on identifying and correcting our character defects. Character defects can be described as ongoing psychological problems. Some of these problems were caused by our addiction itself. Some were present before we ever became addicted.

Our personality problems or character defects can lower the quality of recovery and lead to relapse. To correct our character defects, we must understand what our personality is, and how it operates. On one level, our personality reveals itself in a collection of habits, the sum total of our thinking, feeling, acting, and relating to others. Our personality also reveals itself in automatic thoughts, feelings, and behaviors. We have millions of responses we don't have to think about; they just happen. Some of these are good for us; others are not. If your personality is defined in part by self-defeating or self-destructive habits, these can be identified and worked on in Steps Four through Seven of the Twelve Step program. With these Steps we identify the habits, take responsibility for the resulting behavior, and seek help through our Higher Power and other people in changing that behavior.

Social Health in Recovery

The goal of middle recovery is to learn to function well in family and intimate relationships at work and with friends, and learn to handle the ordinary ups and downs of life. Let's look at these areas.

Family and Intimate Relationships

People who have achieved a healthy and well-balanced family and intimate life are able to communicate openly and honestly with the people they love. If they have a primary relationship, their needs for intimacy, affection, closeness, and sex are met. They are able to let others know who they are, including both their strengths and weaknesses.

Work and Career

In middle recovery, people evaluate their careers, attempt to repair any damage done, and create plans for meaningful and satisfying ways to earn a living. There are two questions to ask yourself:

- Do I have positive relationships with people at work?
- Is my job secure and satisfying?

If you are out of work, it may be a priority to find employment to bring some structure to your life and to feel good about yourself as a productive citizen.

If you are now employed, balanced living requires that you develop job security and job satisfaction. Job security means that you are secure and comfortable in your job. It means you can perform your work responsibilities with competence and that you are not under corrective discipline, on the verge of being fired, or about to be laid off.

Everyone has three possible types of relationships at work: with bosses, peers, and subordinates. Balanced living in the workplace requires that we have positive relationships with these people. It means getting along with our boss and other people who have authority over us. It also means getting along with our peers and other people who have the same level of authority that we do. We also need to get along with our subordinates (people we tell what to do).

To get along with bosses, we must learn to follow instructions. To get along with peers, we need to learn how to cooperate. To get along with subordinates, we have to learn how to give instruction respectfully. In middle recovery, we learn to work effectively with people at all levels.

Job satisfaction means that we like our jobs. We enjoy what we are doing and our work gives meaning and purpose to our lives. Job satisfaction is critical to a productive career. No matter how good you are at a job and no matter how well you get along with people at work, if your job doesn't meet your preferred interests, you eventually get bored and burned out.

Friendships

If we have a balanced social life, we have a network that includes our family, other close friends, and casual friends or associates. We view other people as important and realize that it is possible to have positive relationships with a variety of people. We also take time to be alone, perhaps developing new interests and activities, or just getting to know ourselves better.

Handling Life's Ordinary Ups and Downs

If, in the course of recovery, we often have difficulty managing the ordinary ups and downs and changes that are part of daily living, perhaps you have skipped some of the earlier recovery tasks we've already described. Most of us want to see ourselves as further along in our growth than we really are. We become impatient and try to move ahead as quickly as possible. The result: important recovery tasks remain undone. In A.A., this has often been called "two stepping" which means taking the First Step and skipping immediately to the Twelfth. If you find routine change difficult or demoralizing, go back to the earlier recovery tasks and see if you have really completed them.

Managing Without Chemicals

A very important part of middle recovery is learning how to manage our lives without using chemicals. In middle recovery, we learn our recovery does not necessarily guarantee problem-free living. A stable recovery means we can manage the problems and changes in our lives in an effective manner.

In the Twelve Step program, this is Tenth Step work.

Step 10: Continued to take personal inventory and when we were wrong promptly admitted it.

Working this Step means we have to remain aware of what we are doing and the consequences we will face. At the first sign of a problem, we can acknowledge that something is wrong and take action to correct it. We are learning to solve problems without using chemicals.

As recovering people, we're learning how to separate what we think, what we feel, and what we do. Remembering the letters TFA — THINK, FEEL, ACT — can help. We can think a problem through to its logical conclusion, identify and resolve our feelings, and take positive action.

Recovery skills are developmental. This means that each skill we master makes it possible for us to learn the next. Managing our lives on a day-to-day basis is easier if we have already learned how to think clear and rational thoughts. We know that just because we feel something, doesn't mean we have to act on it. We can use our intellect to determine our emotions and behavior.

When we encounter a problem, we can look within ourselves to see if we have any unresolved feelings such as anger, shame, or guilt that might interfere with our finding a solution. Having identified our feelings, we can begin to resolve them and pursue the solutions to our problem rationally, select an alternative to the best of our ability, and take action if action is needed. We don't have to do this in isolation. We can use close friends or associates as sounding boards. If the problem is too difficult or forces us into an unfamiliar area, we can seek expert advice. This expert advice might need to come from a counselor or therapist.

Why Can't We Find Happiness?

We have attended to the basics of creating a balanced life; it is likely we will encounter other kinds of problems. Remember, recovery is trading one set of problems for another, more manageable set of problems. Many people find that they are able to create some balance in their lives, but they can't maintain it. They appear to be sabotaging themselves by setting themselves up for failure. For example, perhaps we find a person we care about, begin to develop a relationship, and then appear to almost purposely sabotage the relationship. Perhaps we find a good job, but seem to be setting ourselves up to do poorly at it. Perhaps we act responsibly, but we are bored, or anxious, or scared. We have difficulty accepting the good life that we are beginning to have. What's going on here? Why can't we find a happy, productive life even though we appear to have done everything necessary to create it?

The answer can often be found in our family of origin. Many recovering people were raised by alcoholic or dysfunctional parents, and problems created in childhood are haunting them. This happens in the stage I call Late Recovery. In late recovery, we can learn how to be free of our unresolved issues from childhood.

PART VI

Late Recovery — Building Depth and Meaning in Life

We've entered what I call late recovery when, in spite of all the progress we've made, we really don't feel happy. We might be wondering, *Is this all there is to sobriety?*

It's true we're probably doing better than ever before, but even when our lives seem to be going well, there are vague uncomfortable feelings that we can't really identify. Everything seems to check out. We're sober and going to meetings. We have a sponsor and work the program. But we still have a nagging sense that something is wrong. And sometimes it gets the best of us. In spite of all the good things that are happening in our recovery, we lapse into periods of depression, anxiety, frustration, and despair.

Freeing Ourselves from Family Problems

The cause of this unhappiness often has its roots in our family of origin. Many of us grew up in chemically dependent or dysfunctional families, where we learned self-defeating ways of coping with life. These became unconscious habits that we blindly repeated as adults. These self-defeating thoughts, feelings, and behaviors can lower the quality of our recovery and increase the risk of relapse. Late recovery is a time to learn how to free ourselves from the habits, beliefs, and nagging feelings that we learned as children.

Late recovery can be confusing because there are so many different ways of thinking about it. The problems that we experience in late recovery are called by many names. Some people call them family of origin problems. Others who are involved with Adult Children of Alcoholics (ACOA) groups call them *ACA* or *ACOA issues*. Many people lump them under the label *codependency* or *Stage II recovery*. Still others call them therapy or psychotherapy issues. In this chapter, I am going to refer to them as late recovery or family of origin issues.

No matter what we call them, the problems we face in late recovery are usually related to our family of origin. Whether we like it or not, our parents had a powerful effect on our lives. They were our primary teachers during the first ten years of life, when we were most easily influenced by others. We learned about life by observing how our parents lived, related to each other, and treated us. Out of these experiences, we learned what we believed to be the truth about ourselves, others, and the world. I call this "the truth as I see it." We accepted what we learned as true because we had nothing to compare it with. Some of these "parental truths" were accurate. Unfortunately, others were not.

What we learn as children is always a mixed bag. Some parental truths are useful in dealing with the world. Others are not. The problem is that we often don't know which is which. We assume that our basic view of ourselves and others is accurate, and we build our lives around that view. Then we get into trouble, and we don't know why.

If we come from a dysfunctional family, much of what we learn is inaccurate. The "truth as we see it" turns out to be a lie. As a result, we blindly repeat many self-defeating habits that we learned as children. They lower the quality of our recovery and increase our risk of relapse. These habits won't simply go away with sobriety; we need to work at changing them.

Those of us who come from healthy families move through

late recovery quickly and without a great deal of pain. If we were raised in a dysfunctional family, however, the process is more difficult. We often find serious problems that can make our sobriety seem unbearable. To resolve these problems, we have to deal with our family of origin and, to do this, we need to understand the difference between what we learn in a functional and a dysfunctional family.

What a Functional Family Teaches

If we grew up in a functional family, our parents taught us by example that it is safe to honestly look at ourselves and the world around us. We learned that we are basically OK and don't have to pretend we're something we're not. We also learned to honestly experience and talk about what is happening around us. We don't have to pretend that problems don't exist or that things are worse than they really are.

Functional families also teach the benefits of both thinking and feeling. We learn to balance these functions and to use each one appropriately. We learn to think clearly, logically, and rationally. We also learn to identify, describe, and communicate feelings.

As we learned in middle recovery, thinking clearly means that we know what we are thinking and can tell our thoughts to others. Thinking logically means that we use rules to think about and solve problems. When we think logically, one thought does not contradict the other. Logical people feel "together" because their thoughts fit together and do not conflict with each other. Thinking rationally means that our inner thoughts correspond with external reality.

If we came from a healthy family, we developed habits of rational thinking. Because we learned this as children, it became second nature to us. We learned that if something didn't make sense to us, we needed to figure it out. We were taught to believe that it's possible to understand what is really going on. We learned to believe in the power of our own minds to solve problems.

Healthy families teach children the habit of thinking

- clearly (knowing exactly what they are thinking at any given moment);
- logically (thinking thoughts that do not contradict each other); and
- rationally (thinking thoughts that correspond with external reality).

Functional families also teach us to recognize and express our feelings and emotions. We learn that there is no such thing as a good or bad feeling. Feelings simply are. Some feelings are painful but that doesn't make them bad. We learn that pain is a useful signal because, when we are sober, it tells us that something is wrong. Both physical and emotional pain tells us that there is something wrong. Both pleasant and unpleasant feelings have a place in life. Painful feelings can teach us that there is a problem that needs to be corrected. Pleasant feelings can tell us that things are working correctly.

If we come from a functional family, we will bring with us into recovery the ability to think accurately about ourselves, know what we are feeling, and take action in solving problems.

What a Dysfunctional Family Teaches

In a dysfunctional family, we learn ways of thinking that lead to confusion, disorganization, and inner conflict. We learn to believe in ideas that have no basis in reality.

If we came from a dysfunctional family, we probably learned that it is important to remain confused and bewildered. Many of us learned that, if we ever figure out what is really going on, something awful will happen to us. We never learned how to think clearly, logically, and rationally. In fact, many of us learned just the opposite. We came to believe that there are benefits when we think unclear thoughts. We learned that it is normal to have our personal ideas and beliefs contradict each other.

Don't Think about the Reality

Some of us even came to the conclusion that there really is no truth; everything is just a matter of opinion and force. The opinion of the person with the most force is true. For instance, in a family with an alcoholic parent, it is dangerous to think accurately about what is going on. If we talked about what was really happening, our parents would get upset with us and hurt us either physically or emotionally. We came to believe that the whole world was like that.

We may have learned that our thinking doesn't need to match external reality. Reality, we believed, could be anything we wanted it to be. If we didn't like what was going on, we were taught to believe that we could think it out of existence by ignoring or distorting what we saw and heard.

Children in dysfunctional families are frequently punished and abused for telling their parents about the reality of what is wrong with the family. The message given to children in dysfunctional families is, DON'T THINK.

The dysfunctional family teaches that some feelings are good and others are bad. Good feelings are the ones we were allowed to experience because they didn't upset our parents. Bad feelings are those we were taught to fear and repress because our parents didn't know how to deal with them.

Pleasant Feelings = Good   Painful Feelings = Bad . . .

In some types of dysfunctional families, people learn that pleasant feelings are good and painful feelings are bad. As a result, they want to experience only pleasant feelings. They are taught that to experience pain means they are doing something wrong, so pain becomes taboo. They learn to block out the awareness of physical and emotional pain. When they do hurt, they feel guilty, ashamed, and embarrassed. They hide their pain from others because they believe that something awful will happen if others know they are hurting.

. . . or Painful Feelings = Good   Pleasant Feelings = Bad

In some families, children are taught that painful feelings are good and pleasant feelings are bad. They come to believe that there is a nobility in suffering. Only people who suffer are good. Those who relax and enjoy the pleasures of life are evil. As a result, they learn to block out pleasure and focus on the pain and hardship in life. They believe that if they ever feel good, something awful will happen.

Other people learn that all feelings are bad. Good people don't feel; they are cold, calculating, and logical, like Spock in the "Star Trek" television series. To experience any feeling at all is a sign of weakness. If you allow yourself to experience feelings, something awful will happen.

What Happens When We Ignore Our Feelings

In reality, it is natural to feel both pleasant and unpleasant feelings. We are designed to experience emotions. In fact, the more we try to push them away, the stronger they will get. This is simply the way the human emotional system works. If we interpret this to mean that there is something wrong with us, or that something awful will happen if we experience certain types of feelings, we go to war with ourselves. We are forced to disown the feeling part of our nature. As a result, we feel constant stress.

If our family was dysfunctional, having feelings was perceived as wrong or dangerous. So now certain feelings tell us we are defective or unworthy of living; feelings have no place in life; and feelings, or certain kinds of feelings, must be repressed, ignored, or lied about. The overriding message is, DON'T FEEL.

A Delicate Balance

People from functional families balance thinking with feeling. They know it is normal and natural to do both. Normal people see reality, and experience feelings as a result. As they attempt to recognize and communicate their feelings, new thoughts come to mind and the cycle starts all over again. People raised in functional families learn to honor and respect both thinking and feeling. They know that quality living requires the ability to do both. They feel safe and secure in both the world of ideas and the world of inner experience.

Tilting the Balance to Extremes

People from dysfunctional families do not balance thinking and feeling. In an effort to survive, they overidentify with either the thinking function or the feeling function and discount the importance of the other. Some believe TO THINK IS TO BE. They think all the time and use their thoughts to repress feelings and emotions. Others believe TO FEEL IS TO BE. They focus exclusively on their feelings and use them to scatter thoughts.

People from dysfunctional families have little balance between inner and outer awareness. Either the inner world dominates and prevents an accurate awareness of outer reality, or the outer world dominates and prevents awareness of inner reality. Conflict between inner and outer awareness creates an incoherent and contradictory view of self, other people, the world. The person feels torn apart, isolated, alone, and vulnerable. He or she is easily threatened, defensive, and in a constant state of crisis.

Functional families tend to produce people who are capable of realistically appraising themselves, others, and the situations they are in. Dysfunctional families do the opposite by shaping people who are incapable of making accurate assessments. Instead of developing appropriate roles for relating to other people and the world, those from dysfunctional families develop rigid and inflexible survival roles. They cling to these roles as if their lives depended on it, because they believe that it does.

When Are We Ready for Late Recovery?

When should we make family of origin issues the central focus of recovery? People are always asking me how long it takes to get into late recovery. I'm reluctant to give time frames because each of us is so unique. I think it depends upon two things:

- the severity of our addiction, and
- the type of recovery program we use.

The more severe our chemical addiction, the longer it will take for us to move through the earlier stages of recovery. The more intense our recovery program, the sooner we will be ready to tackle our family of origin. I recommend the use of both a Twelve Step program and professional counseling or therapy. If your therapist is skillful in both chemical dependency and family of origin issues, you may progress more rapidly.

I believe we must recognize and accept our chemical addiction before we can resolve our family of origin problems. To focus on family of origin issues too soon can distract us from the chemical addiction and contribute to relapse. Our first job is to get sober. It's important to keep first things first.

I also believe it's best to integrate recovery from family of origin issues with recovery from chemical dependence. In this way, we can safely deal with any family of origin problems that begin to disrupt our sobriety. This is often necessary, especially if we were physically abused, sexually abused, or severely neglected as children.

As a general rule, it's a good idea to keep the primary focus on recovery from chemical dependency during the first year of sobriety. Family of origin issues should only be addressed if they interfere with your ongoing recovery. During the second year, we should deal with the family of origin issues that are fueling the character defects we uncovered during our Fourth and Fifth Steps. After two years of sobriety, most of us will need to deal directly with our family of origin issues if we want to stay comfortably sober. This is especially true if we are experiencing low quality or uncomfortable sobriety, or if we are having numerous relapse warning signs and are afraid we may relapse.

The real tragedy is that there are thousands of chemically dependent people with long-term sobriety who are suffering needlessly because they refuse to deal with family of origin issues.

Common Problems in Late Recovery

Chemically dependent people raised in dysfunctional families face a number of common problems in late recovery. I'll review the ten most common.

Problem 1: Personal Problem Solving

In late recovery, many of us find that we can't solve important personal problems, even though we are able to solve similar problems for other people. We can't seem to think clearly about important personal problems. We can figure out almost anything else. We can fix things when it really isn't important, but we freeze up when it counts.

A recovering alcoholic named Jesse put it this way: "It seems I can figure out how everyone else can solve their problems, but I just can't figure out how to solve mine. At work I'm a genius. Solutions come naturally to me. When I get home and try to figure out what I can do to straighten out my marriage, my mind just goes blank. I feel stupid because I know I'm smarter than that."

Jesse was raised by his mother. His father left when he was three years old, and his mother never got over it. To deal with her pain, she became a professional busybody and people-helper. She was a nurse and helped people through her church activities. Whenever Jesse asked for help, she didn't have time. She told him that he was being selfish in thinking about his own problems; he should think more about helping others and less about helping himself.

Jack is even more confused. He's been sober for five years and working successfully as an accountant. He told me that he is able to manage everyone else's money, but somehow he can't even balance his own checkbook. "I know it's a setup," he told me. "But I just can't manage my money. I know how to do it, but something stops me. It sounds crazy, but I actually get scared or panicked when I start to straighten out my own finances."

Jack's father was a failure. He couldn't succeed at anything. He was constantly going from one failed business venture to another. He couldn't succeed because he wouldn't take care of the details of his life. Jack's mother was disorganized and couldn't keep the house clean, but she made extra money by doing housecleaning for other people. In therapy, Jack told me that he made a commitment as a little kid that he wouldn't be a failure like his father. In spite of that commitment, he can't seem to get it together. He has a good job and makes a lot of money, but he can't seem to manage.

Problem 2: Inability to Manage Feelings

Another common problem is the inability to manage feelings and emotions. Many of us either turn off our feelings, or we overreact.

Jane, who has been recovering for three years, doesn't know what she feels. "It's like I'm numb from the neck down," she says. "I don't feel bad, I don't feel anything. I can enjoy little things in life, but anytime anything important happens I just numb off."

Jane's mother was quiet and reserved. When she was eighteen she fell deeply in love with a man and got pregnant. He walked out on her and she ended up marrying a "very nice" man she didn't love. She constantly told Jane that the way to avoid disappointment was not to get too excited about anything. "If you don't want anything too badly," she told Jane, "you won't get disappointed. Remember what happened to me when I let myself feel too strongly about someone."

Joe has the opposite problem. He overreacts to little things. "It's not everything," he told me. "It's just the things my wife does. At work I can stay cool as a cucumber even when everything hits the fan, but at home the smallest little criticism from my wife sends me into a rage. I always feel guilty afterward, but I can't seem to stop it. Sometimes I think I must be crazy!"

Joe was physically abused by his mother. "She was sweet as pie when Dad was around," he told me, "but watch out when we were by ourselves. I tried to tell Dad about it, but he whipped me for telling lies about Mom. I was so angry I thought I'd explode. But I couldn't. If I ever blew up, I thought she would kill me."

Problem 3: Rigid Habits

Many of us continue to be rigid in spite of years of sobriety. We seem to have trouble changing our behavior even when we want to.

Sarah, with eleven years of sobriety, put it this way: "I don't just get in a rut, I move in and furnish it. It seems I need to keep things in a rigid and unchanging routine. If the routine is ever broken, I feel like I'm going to go nuts. It's not rational, but it's the way I feel."

Sarah's father was a career marine who had a place for everything, and everything was always in its place. If Sarah ever wanted to decorate her room or make it nice, he would laugh at her. "You don't need those silly little girl things," he would tell her. "You're the daughter of a leatherneck. All we need are the basics, and we keep those ready for inspection at all times."

Problem 4: The Need to Take Care of or Rescue Others

Many of us are compulsive people-helpers. We seem almost psychotically devoted to everyone's well-being except our own. We will try to help others when they don't want to be helped. We'll even help others when it hurts us to do so. It seems we just don't feel right about ourselves unless we are busy fixing somebody else's problems. As a result, we often become emotionally involved with people who can't or won't take care of themselves.

Earnie, an alcoholic sober three years, came into therapy when his wife, Theresa, divorced him. When consulted, Theresa told me she was a widow to his drinking and then she became a widow to his recovery. Why wasn't Earnie ever at home? He was too busy sobering up the world.

"I just can't say no," he told me in therapy. "I know I should have been home more, but I just couldn't break away from my meetings. When I saw someone hurting, I felt a need to help them. I couldn't just walk away. And there are a lot of people to help in A.A."

Earnie was an orphan. He has no idea who his parents were. He was left on the doorstep of a social service agency when he was about six months old. He was raised in orphanages and foster homes. No one was ever there when he needed help. He made a commitment to himself when he was a young child that he wouldn't treat other people the way he was treated. He felt a strong need and obligation to help others. His need was so strong that, even though he was sober, he was destroying his own life by giving to others. He never learned to care for himself as an adult because he was never cared for as a child.

Candice is recovering from cocaine dependence. A professional writer in a public relations firm, she had a good job and was a professional businesswoman, but somehow she kept getting involved with unsuccessful men. "I don't understand it," she told me. "I'm an excellent judge of people at work, but when it comes to my love life I seem to check my brain at the door."

Candice had been in five relationships over the first four years of her recovery. Two of these men physically abused her, two verbally and psychologically abused her, and the other man was a professional freeloader who hadn't worked in six years. He was a chronic relapser who periodically drank and then returned to sobriety. Candice describes how she got involved with this man: "I met Jim at a meeting. He said he had no place to live. It was awful cold out and I couldn't let him sleep in the street, so I took him home and let him sleep on my couch. At first it was a roommate situation, but then it became sexual. I wasn't really in love with him, but he was so needy. What could I do?"

As a child in a middle class family, Candice was physically and sexually abused. Her mother worked the night shift as a nurse, and her father worked days as a supervisor in a steel mill. The abuse occurred at night when the mother was gone. After he would sexually abuse her, Candice's father would spank her for tempting him and making him do "those awful things" to her. She never talked about this with anyone, but somehow she found herself attracted to men who would once again abuse her as an adult.

Problem 5: The Need to Quietly Fit in and Do What Others Expect

Many of us get sober and become what I call "grey people." We learn to blend in and not make waves. We do what is expected, but we never do good enough to stand out and be praised or do bad enough to be punished. Some of us become so bland other people don't even know that we are there.

I first became aware of the "grey people" when I was an observer in group therapy in 1969. At the end of one session, the therapist, co-therapist, and I were discussing the group and reviewing progress of the members. "Was Jerry in group this evening?" the therapist asked. None of us could remember. Three professional therapists had met for two hours with a group of ten patients, and none of us were sure if Jerry had attended or not.

Jerry, sixty-two, had been sober for nearly three years. At age forty, he had retired from the army after twenty years. He then got a civil service job at a local military base where he worked as a clerk. He came into therapy because he was depressed but didn't know why. Jerry was divorced before he found recovery and never remarried. He attended four to five A.A. meetings a week, but reported he had no friends. He never had a sponsor and rarely said anything at meetings except, "I'm grateful to be here; I pass." Jerry said he was terrified of standing out. He would switch the meeting he attended every couple of months so people wouldn't get to know him too well.

As a child, Jerry, too, had been physically abused. Anytime he made noise or stood out in any way, he was severely punished. His parents were fundamentalist Christians who believed "children should be seen and not heard" and "spare the rod, spoil the child." He learned it was dangerous to be noticed, and he made a lifestyle out of this principle.

Problem 6: The Need to Entertain Others and Divert Attention from Difficulties

Many of us feel a compulsion to be the center of attention. We can't stand periods of silence at meetings. We get especially uncomfortable when others start to talk about serious or painful problems. To take the pressure off, we begin to joke or clown around.

Linda, thirty-six, had been sober for about four years. She began therapy because she was having serious stomach pains, and her doctor couldn't find any physical reason for the pain. Since she was a recovering alcoholic, she came to our outpatient alcoholism treatment clinic.

Linda was lively and fun to be around. When I first met her for her first session, she had the receptionist laughing at her jokes and was entertaining the other patients in the waiting room. Linda was anything but shy. "Gregarious" or even "rowdy" would be better words to describe her.

She told me she had a lot of friends, regularly chaired and spoke at A.A. meetings, and was very popular. She was single. Her husband left her shortly after she got sober, and she hadn't been able to make a relationship work. "I don't really understand it," she said. "They just seem to lose interest in me after a couple of dates." She then began to tell me jokes that made fun of her loneliness and inability to find someone to love.

In group therapy, Linda was the life of the group, so much so that she was disruptive. The more serious things got, the stronger was her compulsion to tell jokes or shift the focus to herself. She simply couldn't tolerate talking about serious or painful issues.

Linda was raised in an alcoholic home. Both parents drank heavily all through her childhood. "They were fun drunks," she told the group. "Most of the time when they were drinking we had fun together. I was the life of the party. I knew all of the friends. Sometimes they even let me drink with them because I was so funny and entertaining." When problems erupted in the family, it was Linda's job to take the heat off by telling a joke or acting silly. Linda carried this learning with her into recovery.

Problem 7: The Need to Placate and Make Peace at Any Cost

Some of us learn to be placaters. We don't like conflict, so we feel that it's our job to make and keep the peace at any cost. We need to avoid conflict and smooth over hurt feelings. The real problem is we can never take a stand even when we need to do so.

> Elliot was in recovery for over three years when he started attending Adult Children of Alcoholics (ACA) meetings. "I just wasn't happy in my sobriety. It was like there was something missing." He was working a program and things were going well, but he felt anxious and periodically depressed. "It's not that there is anything really wrong," he told me when he first came into therapy. "Everything is really OK; I just don't feel good."
>
> Elliot was the peacekeeper in his family. He learned that it was his job to keep the peace at any cost. Since

his mother and father would have violent arguments, he often felt like a failure. He told me that if he would have tried harder to talk with his mother and father, they wouldn't have fought so often.

When I asked how that relates to his current sobriety, he said he seemed to always be the arbitrator in his family and recovery groups. "Anytime there's a fight or argument, I feel compelled to get in the middle and settle things. Sometimes I tell myself that it's silly and I should stop doing it, but I just can't. I feel like if I don't intervene, things will just get out of hand."

When I asked how he handled things when he was upset, he told me it was better not to make waves. Why ruffle feathers when you don't have to? "Besides," he said, "if you really get angry, you're going to get drunk, aren't you?" Elliot learned as a child that the expression of anger was a dangerous thing, and that it was his job to protect others from it. He carried that belief with him into recovery.

Problem 8: The Need to Accept Blame for the Problems of Others

Many of us are willing to be scapegoats for others. We feel so bad about ourselves that, when others blame us for things, we can't seem to defend ourselves.

Elliot was a scapegoat as well as a placater. When he would attempt to settle an argument, he would willingly accept the blame. "Why not?" he asked. "The goal is to stop the argument."

Problem 9: The Need to Act Out, Break Rules, and Cause Trouble

Some of us are compulsive rule breakers. We don't see anything wrong with it, and we just don't want other people to tell us what to do. We can see that rules may be necessary for other people, but we ask ourselves, *Why should I have to follow them?* We feel entitled to special treatment and don't understand why others get upset with us.

Jake was like this. He had earned the nickname "the snake" when he was in high school. Jake grew up in the Northwest and worked as a longshoreman for years. When he got sober, he didn't feel he had to change anything. He started going to meetings but didn't like the Higher Power stuff. "I'm not going to turn my will and life over to anyone but myself." Jake was in and out of the program for three years, had several relapses, and finally moved to Chicago and settled into regular meeting attendance. He put together two and one-half years of sobriety before he began questioning his values.

"I've never been much for morality," he told me in a counseling session. "I always figured life was what you could get away with, but I'm not sure now that's a good way to live." When Jake wanted to do something and there was a rule or a law against it, he would ask himself two questions before deciding to do it:

- What's the punishment?
- What's the likelihood of getting caught?

If he felt he probably wouldn't get caught, he would do it.

Jake grew up in a family with eleven children. His mother was home, but there just wasn't enough of her to go around. His father was a petty criminal who would brag about his crimes. "My dad taught me that only cowards live by the rules," Jake told me. "If I wanted to be a real man, I'd learn how to live my life on my own terms and to hell with everyone else."

That's how Jake lived for the first years of sobriety. He found himself alone and cut off from others. No one trusted him. He didn't trust the friends he had.

Jake, like many of us, carried his family problems with him after he got sober.

Problem 10: The Need to Blame Others for Your Own Problems

Many of us find it difficult to accept responsibility for our own problems. If something goes wrong, we tend to blame it on someone else.

> This was Jake's style. When he got caught for breaking a rule or law, he would blame the person who caught him. A typical response would be, "What right did that cop have to give me a ticket for speeding?" He would never consider that he was responsible for the consequences of his behavior. If things didn't go right, it was always someone else's fault.

These ten problems of late recovery have two things in common. First, they are all related to what was learned in our family of origin. Second, we feel compelled to continue to act out these problems even though we know better. We can't seem to stop. It's as if we are out of control.

The relationship between these late recovery problems and the family of origin is obvious when we think about it. The problem is we often don't think about it. Many of us come to believe that all of our problems are caused by our chemical dependence, and that all of our problems can be solved by going to meetings and working the Steps. Unfortunately, that's not always true. Unless we identify and decide to solve these late recovery problems, they won't change.

In the Twelve Step program, no specific Steps are designed to resolve late recovery issues. In 1935 the founders of A.A. did not know about the extensive effect childhood experience could have on adult living. Many recovering people do indirectly resolve those family of origin issues while they are working Steps Four and Five and the spiritual program described in Steps Eleven and Twelve. For most, however, these problems will linger unless they are specifically addressed.

A Twelve Step program called Adult Children of Alcoholics helps people identify their family of origin issues. Many ACA members are recovering chemically dependent people with many years of sobriety. They discovered that A.A. alone was insufficient to resolve the problems lingering from their childhood. By working the ACA program in addition to their A.A. program, they can resolve these childhood issues and improve the overall quality of their recovery.

The Late Recovery Questionnaire

Let's look at these ten problem areas and try to personalize them. Below are ten statements which correspond to the ten major problems of late recovery we just discussed. Think about how often you experienced each behavior as a child, and how often you currently experience it at home and at work. Then ask yourself if this is a problem you feel you need to work on in your recovery. Take a few minutes to complete the questionnaire.

1. **Problem solving.** I have difficulty solving important personal problems but am able to solve similar problems for other people.

	VERY OFTEN	SOMETIMES	RARELY
A. As a child	☐	☐	☐
B. Adult (home)	☐	☐	☐
C. Adult (work)	☐	☐	☐

	YES	NO	UNSURE
D. Is this a problem now?	☐	☐	☐

2. **Managing feelings.** I have difficulty managing my feelings and emotions.

	VERY OFTEN	SOMETIMES	RARELY
A. As a child	☐	☐	☐
B. Adult (home)	☐	☐	☐
C. Adult (work)	☐	☐	☐

	YES	NO	UNSURE
D. Is this a current problem?	☐	☐	☐

3. **Rigid behavior.** I have rigid habits that make it difficult for me to change my behavior when I need to.

	VERY OFTEN	SOMETIMES	RARELY
A. As a child	☐	☐	☐
B. Adult (home)	☐	☐	☐
C. Adult (work)	☐	☐	☐

	YES	NO	UNSURE
D. Is this a current problem?	☐	☐	☐

4. **Rescuing.** I rescue or save others to the extent that it causes me problems.

	VERY OFTEN	SOMETIMES	RARELY
A. As a child	☐	☐	☐
B. Adult (home)	☐	☐	☐
C. Adult (work)	☐	☐	☐

	YES	NO	UNSURE
D. Is this a current problem?	☐	☐	☐

5. **Complying.** I quietly fit in by doing what other people expect.

	VERY OFTEN	SOMETIMES	RARELY
A. As a child	☐	☐	☐
B. Adult (home)	☐	☐	☐
C. Adult (work)	☐	☐	☐

	YES	NO	UNSURE
D. Is this a current problem?	☐	☐	☐

6. **Entertaining.** I entertain others in order to divert attention from problems.

	VERY OFTEN	SOMETIMES	RARELY
A. As a child	☐	☐	☐
B. Adult (home)	☐	☐	☐
C. Adult (work)	☐	☐	☐

	YES	NO	UNSURE
D. Is this a current problem?	☐	☐	☐

7. **Peacemaking.** I must assure that there is peace at any cost.

	VERY OFTEN	SOMETIMES	RARELY
A. As a child	☐	☐	☐
B. Adult (home)	☐	☐	☐
C. Adult (work)	☐	☐	☐

	YES	NO	UNSURE
D. Is this a current problem?	☐	☐	☐

8. **Self-sacrificing.** I tend to accept the blame for the problems of others.

	VERY OFTEN	SOMETIMES	RARELY
A. As a child	☐	☐	☐
B. Adult (home)	☐	☐	☐

		YES	NO	UNSURE
C. Adult (work)	☐	☐	☐	☐
D. Is this a current problem?		☐	☐	☐

9. **Troublemaking.** I make trouble by acting out and tend to disrespect or break rules.

	VERY OFTEN	SOMETIMES	RARELY
A. As a child	☐	☐	☐
B. Adult (home)	☐	☐	☐
C. Adult (work)	☐	☐	☐

	YES	NO	UNSURE
D. Is this a current problem?	☐	☐	☐

10. **Blaming.** I tend to blame others for problems that I have.

	VERY OFTEN	SOMETIMES	RARELY
A. As a child	☐	☐	☐
B. Adult (home)	☐	☐	☐
C. Adult (work)	☐	☐	☐

	YES	NO	UNSURE
D. Is this a current problem?	☐	☐	☐

You can look at your answers more closely by taking a sheet of paper and making an answer sheet (see the following). This answer sheet has a place to enter the answer to each question. Use the following scales:

Very Often = 3; Sometimes = 2; Rarely = 1.

For question "D"—"Is this a current problem?"—Y = Yes; N = No; U = Unsure.

	As a Child (A)	At Home (B)	At Work (C)	Current Problem (D)
1. Problem Solving	_____	_____	_____	Y N U
2. Managing Feelings	_____	_____	_____	Y N U
3. Rigid Behavior	_____	_____	_____	Y N U
4. Rescuing	_____	_____	_____	Y N U
5. Complying	_____	_____	_____	Y N U
6. Entertaining	_____	_____	_____	Y N U
7. Peacemaking	_____	_____	_____	Y N U
8. Self-sacrificing	_____	_____	_____	Y N U
9. Trouble-making	_____	_____	_____	Y N U
10. Blaming	_____	_____	_____	Y N U

The answer sheet will allow you to see the roles that you played as a child very clearly. People who come from a dysfunctional family usually find they use one or two roles almost all of the time. People who have entered a recovery process find the scores from childhood are different from their scores in their current family or relationship and on the job.

A person from a functional family would find that he or she answered "sometimes" or "rarely" to almost all of the questions. Why? These are maladaptive roles that are learned in a dysfunctional family. If you come from a healthy and functional family, you would not have learned to frequently use any of these strategies for coping.

Problem-Solving Strategies

Solving the problems of late recovery requires change. A good way to start the process is to identify the unhealthy behaviors associated with family of origin problems and begin to practice healthy behaviors.

Problem solving. People with difficulty solving their own problems need to get into personal therapy, where they can focus on those issues and get support in resolving them.

Managing feelings. People with trouble recognizing and managing their feelings need to learn skills in this area. If we emotionally overreact, we need to recognize the triggers that set off the reaction and then learn other responses. If we tend to become emotionally numb, we must learn how to breath deeply, center ourselves, and notice what's going on inside. We must then learn how to describe those inner feelings and communicate them to others.

Rigid behavior. Those of us who are rigid and have difficulty changing our behavior need to practice flexibility. We need to deliberately schedule activities that will force us out of the ruts we have established for ourselves.

Rescuing. Rescuers need practice at letting others experience their own consequences. In Al-Anon, the skill is called *detachment.* In A.A., it is called *turning it over.*

Complying. Compliers need to practice standing up for themselves. The Twelve Step program is a selfish program. Your sobriety must come first. Life is a selfish process. If you die in the service of others, there isn't much left to share.

Entertaining. Entertainers distract others from the reality of what is going on. They need to learn how to be quiet and let others experience the reality of the situation.

Peacemaking. Peacemakers do almost anything to avoid conflict. They need to learn how to tolerate anger and arguing. They need to stop getting in the middle and trying to fix things.

Self-sacrificing. Self-sacrificers surrender themselves to others. They need to start acting as if they are valuable and worthwhile. They need to stop associating with others who are willing to take advantage of them.

Troublemaking. Troublemakers set themselves up as sacrificial victims. Their chaotic behaviors allow others to view themselves as good by comparison. Troublemakers need to realize that the best way to get back at others is to behave themselves so that other people can't blame them for what is happening.

Blaming. Blamers unfairly blame others for the consequences of their own behavior. They have to learn to look honestly at the consequences of what they do, and learn to acknowledge that they are at fault and take responsibility to clean up the messes they have created.

This all sounds well and good, but what happens if we try to use healthy behaviors and we can't? This is often the case with family of origin issues. We keep the problem behaviors going because we are out of control. We know what to do and we want to do it, but when we try, we feel a strange sense of dread and panic.

> Stan put it this way: "I want to change, I really do, but something seems to stop me. When I stop my caretaking behaviors, I get scared and panicky. In my head, I know there is no good reason for it, but the feeling comes over me anyway. The longer I abstain from the behaviors, the worse the fear gets."

This reaction to change suggests that we may have used the problematic behaviors as survival tools when we were children. Dysfunctional families are dangerous places to grow up. The danger is emotional, physical, or both. But children are survivors. As kids, we quickly learn what to do to minimize the pain and risk. We come to believe that the behaviors that protected us as children will continue to protect us as adults.

We also believe that if we stop using the self-protective behavior, we will get hurt or die. This is what causes the fear and panic when we try to change the behavior.

Let's take a look at Stan. When he was a child, he was severely punished by his alcoholic father for being selfish. His father called him selfish anytime Stan was not actively taking care of his younger brother and sister. Anytime his attention turned from his brothers and sisters and he started taking care of himself, he ran the risk of being humiliated or even beaten. He learned that in order to survive, he needed to care for others. To take care of yourself was dangerous. He internalized this belief and continues to act it out as an adult even though it is no longer true.

If we understand the patterns of survival behaviors we learned as children, it's easier to let go of them as adults.

The Tasks of Late Recovery

If we want to solve the problems of late recovery, we have to be willing to invest the time and energy required. First, we need to recognize that childhood issues are causing us problems in recovery. It's back to Step One, only this time we focus on powerlessness over our childhood.

Second, we'll have to learn something about both functional and dysfunctional families, so we have the background to examine our own childhoods.

Third, we need to reconstruct our childhood history, fill in the gaps in our memory, and discuss what we learn with others who are supportive.

Fourth, we need to make the connection between what we have learned about our childhood and how we are functioning as adults. The key question is, "How am I acting out what I learned as a child in my current life?"

Finally, we need to stop blindly acting out what we learned

as children. We need to break the cycle of family dysfunction by taking responsibility to change who we are and how we act. If we don't change, we will do to our children what our parents did to us.

Task 1: Recognizing Childhood Issues

Many of us have problems from our childhoods that are causing us pain in sobriety. We must learn how to recognize these problems and how they are affecting us. Just as denial initially blocked our awareness of chemical dependency, it can also block our awareness of family of origin problems. At the beginning of late recovery, many of us describe our problems as being one thing after another. As we learn about family of origin problems, we come to see that many of our problems are the result of repeating the same patterns over and over again. It's not one thing after another, but it's the same thing over and over again.

We begin to understand the essence of the Fourth and Fifth Steps, which ask us to identify "the exact nature of our wrongs." These Steps are not just asking us to list specific things we have done wrong. They are asking us to understand "the exact nature" of these problems. This means we need to understand the underlying or core issues that cause the compulsion to repeat these problems. It's not enough to say "I'll never do that again" and use willpower to avoid it.

We must recognize the core problems and accept that it's OK to have them. This acceptance of ourselves as fallible human beings who were affected by our childhoods allows us to resolve the shame, the guilt, and the chronic pain that is fueling our compulsion to repeat the same cycles of self-defeating behavior. This is not only possible, it is necessary if we want to be comfortable with our sobriety.

This means that we explore our childhood to discover the approaches to life we learned as children. We will then be able to make responsible decisions about which attitudes and habits we will keep, and which we will discard. No matter how bad our childhood was, we picked up a combination of strengths and weaknesses. Our continued growth and maturity calls for us to build on the strengths, while working to overcome the weaknesses. The general rule is recover or repeat. Recover from the damage done by our childhood, or repeat the same pattern of self-destructive behavior over and over again.

Task 2: Getting Information

It's important to get accurate information about family of origin problems. We need to learn about the dynamics of both functional and dysfunctional families. We need to know the basics about how habits are formed as children and how those habits can be broken. Reading this book is a beginning, but you will need more than this book provides.

Most treatment programs for adult children of alcoholics have educational programs that provide this information. Many books, audio-, and videotapes can also be helpful.

Task 3: Reconstructing Our Childhood History

Knowledge of how family of origin issues develop is not enough. In recovery, we examine our childhood and talk about it with people who can give us feedback. This process is similar to preparing and telling one's story at A.A.

We develop a written history of childhood, then explain it to others who ask questions and give feedback. As a result, a new understanding of our childhood begins to emerge. We begin to see how the mistaken notions we learned as children have come to affect our lives as adults. Painful memories are recalled and shared with others. The pain and hurt is released and resolved. The shame and guilt is released and resolved. A new sense of freedom is discovered.

Task 4: Connecting Childhood and Adult Problems

The goal of late recovery is to change. I see little value in rehashing out childhood just for the sake of talking about it. Reconstructing our childhood history is most beneficial when we use it to identify patterns of recurring problems that started in childhood that are being repeated in adult living.

Task 5: Lifestyle Change

It is not enough to just examine our childhood. We must consciously connect what we learned as children to how we are conducting life as adults. This is not as easy as it sounds. Our conscious awareness of what we are doing is protected by denial. To break through this denial, we must consciously construct a list of strengths and weaknesses that we developed as children. A conscious plan can then be established for us, as an adult, to recognize and build on these strengths, while recognizing and overcoming the weaknesses.

The completion of this adult self-assessment process based on knowledge of our childhood can be thought about as a modified Fourth, Fifth, and Tenth Step of the A.A. program.

Understanding gives us the promise of change; action turns that promise into reality.

Change in behavior is a critical step in resolving the family of origin issues to change the habitual patterns of thinking, feeling, and acting that are lowering the quality of our sobriety. Deeply ingrained habits will not disappear simply because we understand how they developed. Understanding gives us the promise of change; action turns that promise into reality. This requires setting goals, developing action plans, and enlisting the help of others to support us in our process of recovery.

Finding New Behaviors that Fit

If we come from a dysfunctional family, we have learned to use behaviors that don't fit us very well. We learned a variety of habits that allowed us to get by in life, but didn't make us happy. When we find behaviors that fit us, they feel natural, easy, and free-flowing. These new behaviors give our lives meaning and purpose.

Once we have become free of our childhood, we can find behaviors that fit. We can discover what it is we truly value and find the courage within us to focus our lives around those values. We find these new behaviors by honestly examining our strengths and weaknesses. We strive to honestly answer a number of questions:

- What am I good at?
- What do I like to do?
- How can I contribute to the world?
- What can I do that is meaningful?
- What is my purpose in life?

Answering these questions can become the central focus of the spiritual part of our program.

I believe that everyone was created with a purpose. We are not here by accident. There is something important for us to do with our lives, and it is the responsibility of each of us to search out that purpose and find the courage to act on it in our lives.

My belief is that God created us as rational animals with the power to think. He created a lawful universe that is organized around the law of consequence. He gave us, as human beings, the power of *volitional consciousness. Volition* means the ability to make decisions and act. *Consciousness* means the ability to be aware of the decisions we make, the actions we take to implement those decisions, and the consequences that result.

Once we get sober, our humanity gives us these capacities. We have all that we need every minute of every day to cope with our sobriety. We can think rationally about our life, make decisions, and take actions. The law of consequences teaches us about whether our actions were appropriate or not. If we make mistakes, as all fallible human beings do, we can learn from those mistakes and change.

We find true joy and meaning in sobriety when we have the courage to seek out behaviors and lifestyles that fit us. I believe we all have a purpose, and that we are meant to experience joy and meaning in fulfilling it. We don't need to suffer by doing things that are not satisfying.

Once we discover what those roles are, it takes courage to reorganize our life around them. But to have meaning and purpose in our life requires that we reorganize our lives around those roles. Simply knowing what our basic integrating role is, is not enough for us to change and feel joy in our lives. We must actually change how we live.

By the end of late recovery, if we have had the courage to proceed along the lines described here, we have identified and reorganized our life around our basic integrating role. This doesn't mean that we are problem-free. Recovery is the process of trading in one set of problems for a better set of problems. The more advanced we are in recovery, the more able we are to cope with problems. Successful recovery does not mean being problem-free; it means being better able to cope with the problems that are presented to us in our recovery without becoming upset. At the end of late recovery, we once again trade in one set of problems for a new set of problems. The new set of problems is called Maintenance.

Pulling It All Together

Let's pull together all of this information about late recovery.

All people learn about themselves, other people, and the world from their parents. Chemically dependent people are no exception. The most powerful learning occurs in people before the age of ten, when they are not capable of questioning what they are taught.

Attitudes and habits are learned unconsciously by imitating

those of our parents. This blind and repetitive imitation develops strong and deeply ingrained habits of thinking, feeling, acting, and relating to others.

People accept this early learning as the truth and judge new experiences by comparing them to those truths that were learned as children.

All children learn a mixture of accurate and mistaken beliefs about themselves, other people, and the world in general from their family of origin. Accurate beliefs correspond to objective reality. Mistaken beliefs do not.

When parents teach more accurate than mistaken beliefs and model constructive habits of thinking, feeling, acting, and relating to others, the children develop a solid foundation for happiness and success. They become prone to experience cycles of productive growth and develop and build depth and meaning to life.

When parents teach more mistaken than accurate beliefs and model self-defeating habits of thinking, feeling, acting, and relating to others, the children develop a poor foundation of happiness and success. They become prone to repeat cycles of self-defeating and destructive behaviors.

Family of origin issues do not cause addiction. Addiction is caused by a combination of genetic susceptibility and the use of alcohol or other drugs. People from both functional and dysfunctional families become addicted.

Healthy families teach that joy and meaning in life are normal, and problems and pain are temporary conditions that must be dealt with. Dysfunctional families teach the opposite. They teach that pain and problems are normal, and periods of joy and meaning are temporary and will eventually give way to more pain and problems.

People from dysfunctional families will need to experience more pain from their addiction in order to recognize that they are sick. This is because they were taught as children that "normal" life is pain. People from healthy families will recognize their chemical addiction earlier.

In sobriety, people return to their preaddictive level of life skills. People from healthy families have a solid foundation of responsibly managing life; this makes their recovery easier. People from dysfunctional families have a poor foundation to build on. Even before they became addicted, their life was a series of deeply ingrained, self-defeating habits. As a result, people from dysfunctional families find it more difficult to recover and tend to be more prone to relapse than someone from a healthy family.

Recovery is possible, but it requires work. We must be willing to examine our childhood history, identify problematic beliefs that we learned as children, and then relate them to recurrent problems we originally experienced as children. Then we must be willing to change.

PART VII

Maintenance — Learning How to Enjoy the Journey

The final period of recovery is Maintenance. It lasts a lifetime. We will need to maintain a continued awareness of our chemical dependency, take an inventory of our behavior on a daily basis, and correct problems as they develop. We must also have a strong commitment to growth. We need to grow in our recovery if we are to stay sober.

During maintenance, the focus of recovery shifts from repairing damage to developing a high-quality lifestyle. It begins when we recognize our freedom from the past. We are no longer crippled by the pain, guilt, and shame of our addiction. We have become free of the self-defeating habits learned in childhood. We are now free to grow and develop. Growing spiritually and improving our relationships with others become priorities.

During maintenance, most of us become involved in working Steps Ten, Eleven, and Twelve of the Twelve Step program. Step Ten gives us the mandate to live responsibly One Day at a Time, recognize mistakes, and take corrective action at the earliest opportunity.

Step 10: Continued to take personal inventory and when we were wrong promptly admitted it

We continued to examine ourselves, our behavior, and the

consequences of our behavior. Whenever we begin to create self-defeating consequences, we recognize it and change the behavior that is causing those consequences.

Step 11: Sought through prayer and meditation to improve our conscious contact with God as we understood Him, praying only for knowledge of His will for us and the power to carry that out.

In other words, Step Eleven tells us to search out our unique meaning and purpose in recovery.

Step 12: Having had a spiritual awakening as the result of these steps, we tried to carry this message to alcoholics, and to practice these principles in all our affairs.

The idea of Step Twelve is, "In order to keep it, we have to give it away."

Maintaining a Recovery Program

The disease is called alcohol-ism, not alcohol-wasm. Our disease is in remission, but it will never be "cured." Without an active and continuous program of growth and development, most of us would fall back into our old patterns of addictive thinking, emotional mismanagement, and self-defeating behavior. No matter how long we are sober, this return of destructive thinking and living patterns can set the stage for relapse.

Our recovery program now will be different from the recovery program we worked during stabilization or early recovery. Now we are busy living a sober life, and many of us can attend fewer Twelve Step meetings. Sometimes recovering people can learn to monitor themselves and their reactions to life so well that they know when they need a meeting. Other people need two to three meetings a week to feel comfortable. For them, a close contact to the lifeline of A.A. or N.A. is essential to peace of mind and ongoing recovery.

Many people fall in between the two extremes. They attend a minimum of one Twelve Step meeting a week that gives them the necessary lifeline of support. A friend of mine, Tom Reeves, who died of cancer in 1987, put it this way: "If you are not willing to invest two hours a week in maintaining your recovery from a fatal disease, you really don't want to stay well." I believe this represents a practical and efficient guideline for most recovering people.

During times of high stress or change, the symptoms of post-acute (long-term) withdrawal or addictive thinking may come back even during maintenance. At the first sign of this, it is important to increase efforts at recovery.

If we had cancer in remission, we would have a professional examination at least once a year. We would set up an appointment at the first sign of symptoms or problems. You don't play games with a fatal disease.

Addiction to chemicals is a fatal disease and should be handled that way. An annual sobriety checkup with a certified alcohol and drug dependence counselor should be a priority. During these checkups, we should review our progress in recovery, talk about any life problems and how we are coping with them, update our relapse prevention plan, and monitor ourselves for any emerging warning signs. This annual sobriety checkup will assure us that we are moving ahead in recovery and not slowly giving way to the subtle early warning signs of relapse.

Effective Day-to-Day Coping

In maintenance, we are not problem-free, but we are learning to manage the problems of ordinary living efficiently. One A.A. member put it this way: "Recovery is nothing but a series of problems strung end to end. We are never free of the problems. I measure my recovery not by how many problems I have, but by how well I manage the problems I do have."

I like to think of humans as problem-solving creatures. We are given minds that are capable of thinking, and we are given challenges in life. Our job is to respond to those challenges. We can respond from a position of self-confidence and self-worth, or we can respond from a position of insecurity and fear.

I was very close to my friend, Tom, when he was dying from cancer. Tom had worked a Twelve Step program and had maintained sobriety for over seven years. One of the last messages he gave to his wife, Judy, before he died was, "Please tell other members of the program that the promises of A.A. do come true. We can cope with our life while sober." Tom faced his cancer and his death with courage and dignity using the Twelve Step principles. The Twelve Step program can see us through even the worst of life's crises.

Continued Growth and Development

The human mind, when free from alcohol and other drugs, is designed to seek truth. Father Martin says that human beings are truth-seeking creatures. As humans, we constantly seek truth; we seek the meaning and the purpose behind what we are doing. This urge to seek truth means that we are rarely satisfied for long with what we know. We constantly strive for more understanding, new challenges, and forward movement in our lives.

We grow and change from the time we are conceived until the time we die. This is just the way we are. We are not free to choose whether or not we grow and change. But we are free to choose the direction of that growth and change.

When we stop growing, a dry drunk is just around the corner. Stress builds up and eventually post-acute withdrawal symptoms emerge, triggering a loss of control and possible relapse. Recovery is a lot like walking up a down escalator: There is no such thing as standing still. Anytime we stop going forward, we go backward.

Over the years of our addiction, we got into the habit of denial and evasion. We believed negative emotional states are normal. We got accustomed to responding to the challenges of life with self-destructive behavior. Our bad habits can be managed, but they never completely go away. At certain times, especially times when we are tired or overburdened, self-defeating tendencies will come back.

For most of us, positive growth and change require constant attention to details. Responsible living requires that we consciously choose our thoughts, our emotions, and our actions. We must take time each day to think about what we are feeling, what we are doing, and how we are relating to others. We remain open to growth, we accept our fallibility, and we do the best we can with what we have.

Coping with Changes and Complications

I used to have a poster of the cartoon character Charlie Brown with a philosophical look and his finger in the air saying, "It's always darkest right before it turns pitch black." Sometimes, it seems the problems in life are never ending. We go through cycles of life. During the first half of life, we are compelled to explore the world outside of us and figure out how it works. Then Mother Nature plays a trick on us. As soon as we become comfortable operating in the external world, we enter the second half of our life, marked by an inward turn, a spiritual journey of self-discovery. During this inward arc, we must consciously integrate the meaning of life with our personal place in the universe. We must come to terms with such vital issues as life, death, and what lies beyond death.

In the late recovery period, we develop a sense of what normal adult development is. We recognize a healthy life requires growth and change. We know that every time we learn and assimilate something, we open up to new learning and growth. We come to anticipate as we grow older. We surrender our youth gracefully while we embrace maturity.

Having once been a Boy Scout, I never forgot the motto, "Be Prepared." Being prepared for our lives as recovering people means learning what to expect as we age, by understanding the experiences of others who have gone before us. We can find role models to communicate with about what may be ahead in the next years of our life. These sponsors or mentors are vital to our growth and development.

One eighty-seven-year-old recovering person told me she always made a point of having two sets of friends. One set of friends were at least ten years older and the other ten years younger. She could remember what it was like to be younger and provide useful counsel to people who are in places she used to be. She could also look ahead and see where she was going. Her only regret at being eighty-seven is that it is difficult to find anyone who is ten years older. She misses having pathfinders out breaking the trail ahead of her. As a result, she feels lonely. She also feels that she is breaking new ground.

Coping with Stuck Points in Recovery

The Big Book of Alcoholics Anonymous (page 60, Third Edition) tells us it is unwise to expect "perfect" adherence to a recovery program. The exact statement is, "We claim spiritual progress rather than spiritual perfection." Each of us will get stuck in our recovery process periodically. This is the most important message I have for you. Getting stuck in recovery is neither good nor bad; it simply is.

Those of us who are successful in recovery cope with our stuck points through a process of recognition and problem solving. We learn how to recognize we are having a problem and are stuck in our recovery. We accept this as OK, knowing as fallible human beings, we reserve the right to make mistakes and encounter problems we don't know how to cope with. We detach from the problem while we seek help from others. Finally, when we are prepared, we take responsible action.

The RADAR Approach to Problem Solving

We can perhaps best remember this process by using the acronym RADAR. The "R" stands for *Recognize*. To Recognize means to know that we are stuck. The first "A" stands for *Accept*. We not only recognize we are stuck, but we also know it is OK; there is nothing to be ashamed about or guilty for. We understand we are fallible human beings who periodically have life problems. The "D" stands for *Detach*. We turn our problems over. This means we back off and gain perspective. The second "A" stands for *Accept help*. We turn to a Higher Power for courage, strength, and hope. We turn to other people for help and support. The final "R" stands for *Respond with action*. Problems just don't go away; we need to solve them. We take positive action to get unstuck.

People who experience low-quality sobriety and eventually relapse cope with stuck points in a very different way. Rather than recognize they are stuck, they evade or deny problems, creating stress. They might deny this stress or blame it on someone or something else. Their stress fuels other compulsive behaviors such as overeating, overworking, overexercising, compulsive sexuality, or codependent relationships. These substitute compulsions or addictions are used to relieve the stress of constant denial, blocking awareness of real problems in recovery.

Substitute compulsions relieve stress in the short run, but weaken people in the long run. People who substitute compulsions to manage stress feel good now, but hurt later. As a result, more stress symptoms develop and get worse.

If we are trying to cope with stress this way, we lock onto the problem, hide it from others, and blindly struggle ahead without thinking. We avoid others and develop new problems resulting from our isolation. We meet every new problem with more denial and evasion. We deny problems. We deny the need to do anything about them. We deny the need for help.

The ESCAPE Style of Coping

The denial/evasion style of coping can be remembered by using the acronym ESCAPE. The first "E" is for *Evasion and denial of the stuck point or problem*. The "S" stands for the *Stress that naturally follows*. The mind is designed to seek truth. Anytime we deny reality we turn our mind off. This takes energy and puts stress and strain on the body. The "C" is for *Compulsive behavior*. Stress causes uncomfortable feelings. Compulsive behaviors temporarily distract us from these feelings. At times, compulsions become so strong that they become addictions. (Never underestimate the great number of people recovering from chemical dependencies who have simply traded chemical addiction for another compulsion.) "A" is for *Avoidance of others*. Compulsive behavior drives others away and we become isolated and alone. "P" is for the *new Problems* that come from stress, compulsive behaviors, and isolation. These problems get worse. The second "E" is for *Evasion and denial of the new problems*, which start the vicious cycle of self-defeating behavior again. Each cycle drains more energy. We weaken until our ability to cope is seriously impaired.

The important thing is to understand about addictive coping. Anytime we choose to cope through denial and drain off our stress through addictive behaviors, it weakens us. I don't think there is such a thing as positive addiction. All addictions are negative because they feel good now and cause pain later. They give us the illusion of strength and confidence, but they lower the quality of our lives and increase our vulnerability to stress and problems.

Putting It All Together

In short, the effective way to cope with problems in sobriety is to turn on our consciousness. When something is wrong, we become aware of it, acknowledge it, and discuss it with others. It is important to examine our history to learn from past mistakes. If we don't learn from history, we are condemned to repeat it. It is important to have a plan of action. What will we do differently in the future? Earnie Larsen puts it well when he says, "If nothing changes, nothing changes." We need to do something different if we are going to grow and change. Most important, we need to focus on what we are doing in the here and now. Abraham Maslow studied healthy, fully functioning people and found them to be time competent. A time-competent person is not trapped in the past, the present, or the future. The time-competent person can move fluidly from present to past, past to present, present to future, and future to present. We tend to spend about 60 percent of our waking consciousness enjoying the immediate here and now. We spend about 40 percent of our time going back into the past or fantasizing about the future. Studying the past helps us to learn from our past experiences, both successes and failures. Fantasizing about the future allows us to develop a viable action plan that will get us there. The attention to the here and now allows us to do what is necessary to bridge the gap between past and future, and to learn how to enjoy the journey.

Epilogue

The passage through recovery is a long and complicated process. But there is a road map. Over the years, we have been able to assemble the stories of thousands of recovering people. Their experiences have shown us the landmarks. They have taught us about the dead ends and treacherous canyons. If we're smart, we can benefit from their directions.

Recovery actually begins with the addiction process itself. As we begin to bottom out on the addiction, we begin to recover. During this transition period, we struggle to control our use and eventually recognize that the only way out is through total abstinence. When we attempt to abstain, we experience both short-term and long-term withdrawal. We must also learn how to deal with the addictive thinking that can lead back to chemical use.

In early recovery, we learn to recognize our addiction as what it is: a chronic, progressive, and eventually fatal disease. We develop a recovery program and begin to resolve the shame, guilt, and nagging pain created by our addictive use. In middle recovery, we make amends by repairing the past damage from our chemical use and then move ahead to create a balanced, comfortable, and meaningful lifestyle. In late recovery, we resolve our family of origin problems and become free from our childhood limitations. In maintenance, we continue our growth and development.

At the start of recovery, many of us felt that our chemical

dependence was a curse. We hated the fact that we couldn't drink and use other drugs like normal people. Somewhere in the process most of us begin to see our recovery as a blessing. By learning how to live the sober life, we learn how to find meaning and purpose. We somehow change and become more than we ever thought we could be.

I hope this book has brought some light into the passageway of recovery. I've tried to share the tools that I have found most useful personally and professionally. No matter how difficult things become, remember that there is hope. People can recover. No matter how far down our chemical addictions have dragged us, we can turn our experiences into helpful tools for others. May you have a good journey on your passage through recovery.

APPENDIX ONE

*THE TWELVE STEPS OF ALCOHOLICS ANONYMOUS**

1. We admitted we were powerless over alcohol — that our lives had become unmanageable.
2. Came to believe that a Power greater than ourselves could restore us to sanity.
3. Made a decision to turn our will and our lives over to the care of God *as we understood Him.*
4. Made a searching and fearless moral inventory of ourselves.
5. Admitted to God, to ourselves, and to another human being the exact nature of our wrongs.
6. Were entirely ready to have God remove all these defects of character.
7. Humbly asked Him to remove our shortcomings.
8. Made a list of all persons we had harmed, and became willing to make amends to them all.
9. Made direct amends to such people wherever possible, except when to do so would injure them or others.
10. Continued to take personal inventory and when we were wrong promptly admitted it.
11. Sought through prayer and meditation to improve our conscious contact with God *as we understood Him,* praying only for knowledge of His will for us and the power to carry that out.
12. Having had a spiritual awakening as the result of these steps, we tried to carry this message to alcoholics, and to practice these principles in all our affairs.

* The Twelve Steps of A.A. are taken from *Alcoholics Anonymous* (Third Edition), and published by A.A. World Services, Inc., New York, N.Y., 59-60. Reprinted with permission.

I. Transition	II. Stabilization	III. Early Recovery
1. Develop motivating problems.	1. Recognition of the need for help.	1. Full conscious recognition of addicitve disease.
2. Failure of normal problem-solving.	2. Recovery from immediate after-effects.	2. Full acceptance and integration of the addiction.
3. Failure of controlled use strategies.	3. Interrupting pathological preoccupation.	3. Learning nonchemical coping skills.
4. Acceptance of need for abstinence.	4. Learning nonchemical stress management methods.	4. Short-term social stabilization
	5. Developing hope and motivation.	5. Developing a sobriety-centered value system.

(Start of Relapse Process)

Coping With Stuck

1. Denial and evasion:
   (The relapse-prone style)
   a. **E**vade/deny the stuck point.
   b. **S**tress.
   c. **C**ompulsive behavior.
   d. **A**void others.
   e. **P**roblems.
   f. **E**vade/deny new problems.
      MEMORY PEG = ESCAPE

High-Risk Factors	Trigger Events	Internal Dysfunction
1. High-stress personality.	1. High-stress thoughts.	1. Difficulty in thinking clearly.
2. High-risk lifestyle.	2. Painful emotions.	2. Difficulty in managing feelings and emotions.
3. Social conflict or change.	3. Painful memories.	3. Difficulty in remembering things.
4. Poor health maintenance.	4. Stressful situations.	4. Difficulty in sleeping restfully.
5. Other illness.	5. Stressful interactions with other people.	5. Difficulty in managing stress.
6. Inadequate recovery program.		6. Difficulty with physical coordination.
		7. Shame, guilt, hopelessness.
		8. Return of denial

Recovery: The Relapse/Recovery Grid
T. Gorski Copyright, T. Gorski, 1987 (Revised May 1987)

IV. Middle Recovery	V. Late Recovery	VI. Maintenance.
1. Resolving the demoralization crisis.	1. Recognizing the effects of childhood problems on sobriety.	1. Maintain a recovery program.
2. Repairing addiction-caused social damage.	2. Learning about family-of-origin issues.	2. Effective day-to-day coping.
3. Establishing a self-regulated recovery program.	3. Conscious examination of childhood.	3. Continued growth and development.
4. Establishing lifestyle balance.	4. Application to adult living.	4. Effective coping with life transitions.
5. Management of change.	5. Change in lifestyle.	

Points In Recovery

2. Recogniton and problem solving:
   (The recovery-prone style)
   a. **R**ecognizing a problem exists.
   b. **A**ccept that it is okay to have problems.
   c. **D**etach to gain perspective.
   d. **A**sk for help.
   e. **R**espond with action when prepared.

   MEMORY PEG = RADAR

(Return of the Recovery Process)

External Dysfunction	Loss of Control	Lapse/Relapse
1. Avoidance and defensive behavior.	1. Poor judgment.	1. Initial use of alcohol or other drugs.
2. Crisis building.	2. Inability to take action.	2. Severe shame, guilt, and remorse.
3. Immobilization.	3. Inability to resist destructive impulses.	3. Loss of control over use.
4. Confusion and overreaction.	4. Conscious recognition of the severity of loss of control.	4. Development of health and life problems.
5. Depression.	5. Option reduction.	
	6. Emotional or physical collapse.	

CENAPS Corporation, PO Box 184, Hazel Crest, IL 60429, 312-335-3606

SUGGESTED READING

Alcoholics Anonymous. *Alcoholics Anonymous* (The Big Book, Third Edition). New York: Alcoholics Anonymous World Services Office, 1976.

Black, Claudia. *It Will Never Happen to Me.* Denver: M.A.C. Publishing, 1981.

Downing, Cynthia. *Triad—The Evolution of Treatment For Chemical Dependence.* Independence, Mo. Independence Press, 1989.

Earll, Bob. *I Got Tired of Pretending.* Tucson, Ariz.: Stem Publishing, 1988.

Gorski, Terence T. *The Relapse/Recovery Grid.* Center City, Minn.: Hazelden Educational Materials, 1989.

_____. *The Twelve Steps—A Guide For Counselors and Therapists.* Independence, Mo.: Independence Press, 1989.

_____. *The Staying Sober Workbook: A Serious Solution For The Problem of Relapse.* Independence Press, 1988.

_____. *Staying Sober—A Guide For Relapse Prevention.* Independence, Mo.: Independence Press, 1986.

_____. *Denial and Confrontation In Recovery: A Workshop Manual.* Hazel Crest, Ill.: The CENAPS Corporation, 1984.

Gorski, Terence T. and Merlene Miller. *Mistaken Beliefs About Relapse.* Independence, Mo.: Independence Press, 1986.

Kritsberg, Wayne. *The Adult Children of Alcoholics Syndrome: From Discovery to Recovery.* Pompano Beach, Fla.: Health Communications, 1985.

_____. *Chronic Shock and Adult Children of Alcoholics.* Pompano Beach, Fla.: Health Communications, 1985.

Larsen, Earnie. *Stage II Relationships: Love Beyond Addiction.* San Francisco: Harper and Row, 1987.

_____. *Stage II Recovery: Life Beyond Addiction.* San Francisco: Harper and Row, 1985.

Martin, Father Joseph C. *The Twelve Steps of Alcoholics Anonymous: Some Personal Comments On The Most Effective Therapy On Earth.* Aberdeen, Md.: Kelly Productions Inc., 1984.

_____. *No Laughing Matter: Chalk Talks about Alcohol.* San Francisco: Harper and Row, 1982.

Miller, Merlene, Terence T. Gorski, and David K. Miller. *Learning To Live Again: A Guide To Recovery From Alcoholism.* Independence, Mo.: Independence Press, 1982.

Miller, Merlene and Terence T. Gorski. *Family Recovery: Growing Beyond Addiction.* Independence, Mo.: Independence Press, 1982.

Narcotics Anonymous World Service Office. *Narcotics Anonymous* (Fourth Edition). Van Nuys, Calif.: World Service Office, Inc., 1987.

Rosellini, Gayle and Mark Worden. *Strong Choices, Weak Choices: The challenge of Change in Recovery,* Center City, Minn.: Hazelden Educational Materials, 1988.

Wegscheider, Sharon. *Another Chance: Hope and Health For Alcoholic Families.* Palo Alto, Calif.: Science and Behavior Books, 1981.

Wuertzer, Patricia and Lucinda May. *Relax, Recover: Stress Management for Recovering People.* Center City, Minn.: Hazelden Educational Materials, 1988.

INDEX

W

Other titles of interest . . .

The Dry Drunk Syndrome
by R.J. Solberg

What is the dry drunk syndrome and why is it important that you know what it is? Discover the answers in this easy-to-understand pamphlet. You'll learn what the dry drunk syndrome is, its common traits, typical family reactions, the necessity for outside help, and preventive measures you can take to avoid this syndrome. Pamphlet, 22 pp.
Order No. 1251

Coming Back from a Relapse
by Sherry Schultz

A Hazelden *Recovery Issues* Workbook

An excellent resource to reaffirm the progress you've made in your recovery and better understand how and why you experienced a relapse. *Coming Back from a Relapse* helps you identify relapse warning signs, establish a practical relapse prevention plan, and learn ways to avoid self-defeating reactions. Workbook, 33 pp.
Order No. 5374

Things My Sponsors Taught Me
by Paul H.

Paul H. brings together A.A. philosophy, quotes, slogans, and refreshing reminders about living without alcohol or other drugs in a reference you'll come back to again and again. You'll find yourself nodding in agreement, chuckling, and anticipating the next bit of wisdom. Paperback, 76 pp.
Order No. 5155

Strong Choices, Weak Choices
by Gayle Rosellini and Mark Worden

This easy-to-read, easy-to-understand pamphlet provides basic information on how to create a sober life. Stories illustrate the benefits of making healthy choices in our lives and recovery. Pamphlet, 24 pp.
Order No. 1325

For price and order information, or a free catalog, please call our Telephone Representatives.

HAZELDEN

1-800-328-0098
(Toll Free. U.S., Canada and the Virgin Islands)

1-612-257-4010
(Outside the U.S. and Canada)

1-612-257-1331
(24-Hour FAX)

Pleasant Valley Road • P.O. Box 176 • Center City, MN 55012-0176